14th HEAVY BATTERY
R.G.A.
WAR DIARY

BATTERY STATIONED AT NEIDERZIER, GERMANY. JANUARY, 1919.

To face title page.

14th HEAVY BATTERY R.G.A.

WAR DIARY

LIST OF HONOURS AND AWARDS TO OFFICERS, N.C.O.'s AND MEN WHILST SERVING WITH THE

BATTERY

LIST OF OFFICERS WHO HAVE SERVED
WITH THE BATTERY
and
BATTERY ROLL OF HONOUR

LONDON: ROBERT SCOTT
ROXBURGHE HOUSE
PATERNOSTER ROW, E.C.
MCMXIX

Foreword

A FEW words regarding the general work of the Battery may be of interest. When so much has happened, the difficulty is to remember all the incidents which ought to be mentioned, and many names and deeds worthy of great reward must go unrecorded. The "Honours List" and "Roll of Honour" given in the Battery Diary will be the only record of many.

Until the battle of the Somme (1916) the Battery had a comparatively easy time and sustained few casualties, but Sergt. Everett (then Gnr.) had gained the first honour by winning the M.M. under very creditable circumstances.

For the Somme we got 60-pounders, and a very early incident of the battle was 2nd Lieut. Sanders being wounded and the bravery of Bdrs. Adams and Muir, who carried him to the dressing station; but, all things considered, we were very lucky during the whole battle from July till January, 1917. We felt the loss of Lieut. Mullis keenly, and knew he was one of the best officers we ever had; and 2nd Lieut. Denison, although only with us a short time, was very popular and gave promise of becoming a worthy officer when unfortunately he was wounded and gassed.

Being on the extreme left flank of the battle, we had an easier time than some batteries; but at the guns we had lots of firing both by day and night, and no one had two consecutive nights in bed for some months, while at the horse-lines life was about as uncomfortable as it could be. The two feet or so of mud which covered the countryside, and incidentally most of the horses and drivers, killed many of the former and nearly broke the hearts of the latter. Ammunition supply was by limbered wagon in those days, and the drivers and horses had a very hard time.

We all remember how we left the Somme and the exhausted state of horses and men after the first day's march, but we soon picked up when we got to Arras, and were ready for the battle of Arras on April 9, 1917. That was a great day, and we were the first heavy battery up the Cambrai road, although many people do not believe it.

The following few weeks were awful. Those nights when we were in action just on the right of the road near Maison Rouge, each have a record of casualties in killed and wounded. I think we may be proud of the way the gunners, and all concerned, behaved during what was probably one of the most trying fortnights in the life of the Battery. Moving to Wancourt did not improve matters much, and we lost Major Pearson wounded, whom we all liked. But it was here that Major Watson joined us, and we know that his taking over command marked a new epoch in our history.

We had just come through a very trying time. We had lost about thirty casualties in twenty days. Major

Watson came from an old regular battery, and when he joined 14 H.B. he found we had our faults; but we must put it on record that what impressed him most of all was the fact that we could shoot, and Major Watson had been an Observation Officer for two years and knew what shooting was. Nevertheless, after our recent experiences we needed pulling together, and our new O.C. did it.

What a great relief it was when we finally got out of the Wancourt position! The gunners had had very hard work and almost constant shelling to put up with. The O.P. party had had lots of fun in the shooting, but some of them will not easily forget one or two of their journeys to and from the O.P. The drivers had much hard work to do to improve the condition of the horses after the Somme and the hard winter, and also they came in for some attention from the Hun long range guns.

The next position, on the left of the Cambrai road near Feuchy Chapel corner, was one of the pleasant incidents. No casualties and a good O.P. and any amount of observed shooting on the Drocourt-Queant line which the Huns were just building. Probably it was the best sport we ever had, and must have annoyed the Bosche considerably.

The fortnight at Point du Jour was only an incident, and then we moved up to the coast for real business again. The five months we were there severely tested the Battery, but we made something of a reputation. It is no exaggeration to say we were shelled almost continuously—we had only two definite strafes on us, but every night and periodically during the day we experienced shell storms and harassing fire. The casualty list steadily grew. We shall never forget 2nd Lieut. Peggie and 2nd Lieut. Purdie, both killed in one night. Many N.C.O.'s and men were killed or wounded, not only at the guns, but the wagon-lines also came in for much shelling and bombing, and added several names to our Roll of Honour. But there was a brighter side and many acts of gallantry were performed, the Battery receiving several honours and awards. Mention must be made of the O.P. party, under Capt. Spalding (then Lieut.), who did excellent work and kept a system of cross observation going under most difficult circumstances, and every credit must be given them, especially the linesmen, who had a very strenuous time. We also remember the new potatoes and vegetables, and the horses should remember the grass which "Lyddite" cut. The result was that we pulled out with horses in excellent condition, and went to a well-deserved rest.

From that time on, the wagon-lines held a prominent position in the Battery, and in the 92nd Brigade we achieved a reputation for our horses as well as for our gunnery.

In the March, 1918, show we have much to be proud of; for although we did nothing very startling, our discipline and coolness never deserted us, and we were always ready and able to do everything we were called upon to do. And so with plenty of firing both by day and night, and fortunately with few casualties, we went through the early summer of 1918 and were ready for the great advance which, for us, began on August 21. How well everything went in the Battery! Every one knew his job and what was expected of him, and under Major Watson's able guidance we could change our position with the minimum of worry and fatigue. The O.P. party had plenty of work, and they did it well; and the gunners and drivers worked together with such system that in spite of constant move and any amount of work, everything went smoothly until the great and glorious end.

Now it's all over, various incidents are remembered by each of us with joy or pride. There has been some sadness in our lines during the past few years, but I cannot think of any portion of the Battery's history of which we need not be proud, and our sorrows were tempered by the bravery and unselfishness which often accompanied them. It is impossible to record all the acts of courage and devotion to duty, but we must remember that the reputation of the Battery has been gained by the good work of all.

The earlier O.C.'s did much in training the Battery for the great battles which began with the Somme. Captain Wiltshire brought the shooting up to a high standard; Major Pearson was O.C. for a short time only, but improved our material and horse-lines. Major Watson has done wonders for us, and we are all agreed that we could not have had a better O.C. for the warfare of the last two years.

And above everything, let us not forget those who gave most of all, and laid down their lives for their country in the service of 14 Heavy Battery.

LIST OF PLATES

The Battery at Niederzier		*Facing title*
Battery Staff absent from Large Group.	*Facing page*	15
Lieut. (now Capt.) E. W. Spalding, M.C.	,, ,,	39
N.C.O.'s and Men who remained with the Battery from May, 1915, to February, 1919	,, ,,	45
2nd Lieut. A. W. B. Peggie	,, ,,	52
Battery Position, Souastre Fork	,, ,,	60
Officers of the Battery, November, 1918	,, ,,	80
Map showing Positions where the Battery was in Action, etc. (*Drawn by Lieut. W. J. Baird, M.C.*)	,, ,,	107

GROUP OF THE BATTERY STAFF UNAVOIDABLY ABSENT ON DUTY WHEN LARGE PHOTO WAS TAKEN.
NEIDERZIER, GERMANY APRIL, 1919.

WAR DIARY

October, 1914

Battery was formed by Lord Kitchener in August or September, and was originally 8 Heavy Battery, being the first heavy battery raised after beginning of War. First postings of N.C.O.'s were to 8 Heavy Battery.

About beginning of October unit became 14th Heavy Battery.

Oct. 3. Battery first appeared as such about this date on Woolwich Common. Consisted of Lieutenant Reid and some twelve regular and re-enlisted N.C.O.'s only.

The other five batteries of 1st New Army were similarly situated.

Oct. 15. Personnel posted, mostly from Newhaven Depot, to Battery about this time.

Major C. W. Collingwood commanded Battery for a few days.

Oct. 18. Major Taylor joined about this time, and obtained two 4·7 guns for training purposes.

Captain Niven and 2nd Lieut. J. R. Davies joined.

Oct. 26. Lieut. Reid posted away. Also Major Taylor.

Oct. 27. 2nd Lieut. J. F. Young joined.

Oct. 28. Major C. N. Buzzard joined. Captain Niven posted to command 10 Heavy Battery, also on Common (29th).

Oct. 30. 2nd Lieut. C. W. D. Ward and 2nd Lieut. D. I. Thomson joined.

Among the N.C.O.'s during this month were B.S.M. Leader, B.Q.M.S. McVeigh, Sergeants Louch, Hewitt, Cooper, Thomson and Luke.

All personnel were accommodated in tents.

November, 1914

Nov. 1. Training begins seriously under Major Buzzard.

2nd Lieut. J. R. Davies, with Sergt. Louch, began the training of the B.C. Staff, mostly on Shooter's Hill and Blackheath.

The Nos. 1 were allotted and practice was carried out on the two guns.

The Major, with Q.M.S. McVeigh, continued systematically to collect the equipment for the Battery.

Nov. 7. Forty H.D. horses, ten cobs allotted to Battery with collar harness and saddles.

Riding classes were formed forthwith, and saddlery was fitted by Saddler Sergt. Henderson.

Sections were allotted as follows:—
Right Section: 2nd Lieut. Young.
Left Section: 2nd Lieut. Ward.
A.C. Section: 2nd Lieut. D. I. Thomson.
B.C. Staff: 2nd Lieut. J. R. Davies.

The horses at this time were all picketed down with ground rope and heel shackles. Nose-bags were not allowed to be used owing to the prevalence of catarrh.

Nov. 10–25. During this period guns were often out, with B.C. Staff, etc., training around the area. At this time no G.S. wagons were allotted.

Very heavy rains about the 20th, making the ground for the horses very bad indeed.

Nov. 27. About this date conditions became so bad that Battery was moved to Charlton Park (the Deer Park).

Nov. 28. Captain Smythe joined. Major Buzzard left to command 90 H.B.

Nov. 30. Some eight G.S. wagons allotted about this date. These were immediately used for fetching clinker and brushwood for constructing roads into the Park.

Horse standings were made from loads of sawdust and wood shavings from the Arsenal.

Captain H. Wilson joined.

December, 1914

Dec. 3. Captain Smythe promoted Major and leaves for Coast Defence.

Major Evan-Smith joins.

Due to the numerous fatigues, training was hampered, and, moreover, guns could not be moved about, due to the mud.

Dec. 7. Lieut. Gilling joins about this time.

Dec. 10–24. During this period trouble was experienced with the horses, catarrh and pneumonia being very prevalent.

Dec. 24–31. Christmas passed off well, and during this period all the personnel got four days' leave, 50 per cent. at a time.

January, 1915

JAN. 5. About this date all personnel was moved into huts in another part of the Park, horses remaining where they were, as stables were not ready.

JAN. 7. Lieut. Gilling posted away.

JAN. 10. Lieut. Boys joined and took over Right Section.
Guns were moved on to one of the gun parks near Wellington Barracks, and detachments were marched down each day for training.
2nd Lieut. Davies to 90 H.B. 2nd Lieut. Young to B.C. Staff.

JAN. 11–25. Training continued steadily, though, due to the bad conditions, guns were not often out.

JAN. 26. Major Evan-Smith leaves and relinquishes his commission. Captain Wilson temporarily in command.

JAN. 30. Horses moved into covered stables close to huts. Guns moved up near stables.

February, 1915

FEB. 1–6. Nothing of note during this period, except that Lieut. Boys joins 71 H.B., mobilizing for France.

FEB. 7. 2nd Lieut. D. I. Thomson goes with billeting party to Merrow, near Guildford.
Lieut. W. J. O. Studd and 2nd Lieut. Eastwick-Field join.

FEB. 8. Battery moves by train from Woolwich to Guildford, thence marches to quarters in Clandon Park, Merrow.
2nd Lieut. O. I. Thomson posted to Coast Defence.

FEB. 11. Major R. A. Thomas joins.
Officers as follows:—
Right Section: Lieut. W. J. O. Studd.
Left Section: 2nd Lieut. Young.
B.C. Staff: 2nd Lieut. W. L. Eastwick-Field.
A. Column: 2nd Lieut. C. W. D. Ward.

The Headquarters of the Battery were at Temple Court, in Clandon Park. Horses, vehicles and guns (two) were accommodated in the Park.

Officers were billeted with Colonel Sykes (R.E. retired), Colonel Browell (R.A. retired), and Mr. Collins (I.C.S. retired).

FEB. 21–28. Training continued steadily.

Battery was made up to some 120 H.D. horses during this time, but the remounts were very poor, and spread lice and ringworm in the Battery for a time.

March, 1915

MAR. 1–7. Practice went on around Guildford.

MAR. 7. 2nd Lieut. Young leaves for fourteen days in France with 24 Heavy Battery, in action then, one section at Le Bizet (north of Armentiéres), and the other behind Bois Crenier (south of Armentiéres).

MAR. 29. Battery travels by road to Aldershot, and moves into tents at Camp 37, Bourley Road.

April, 1915

APRIL 4–10. Made up full strength in horses and vehicles about this time. 60-pounder guns not yet ready for Battery, and two 4·7 guns added to complete temporary equipment.

APRIL 12–16. Divisional manœuvres (14th Division) round Farnham, Winchfield, Fleet, etc., consisting of operations against the 12th Division.

Battery was billeted in whatever area it was directed to by the Staff in accordance with the operations.

Blank charges were used to a limited extent.

WAR DIARY

APRIL 20–27. Several long route marches with other units of the Division, also forced marches, in all of which a time-table had to be rigidly adhered to, took place during this period.

APRIL 28. Battery marches to Larkhill, Salisbury Plain, for firing practice with the 4·7 guns (though 60-pounders were still expected), taking three days to do journey.

2nd Lieut. Young stays with Q.M.S., etc., to complete equipment from Ordnance, Aldershot. Other officers proceed with Battery.

May, 1915

MAY 7. Battery returns from Larkhill (after successful practice shooting) by rail to Farnborough.

MAY 8–19. Preparing for active service. Personnel goes on last leave (three days) before embarking.

MAY 20. Entrain at Aldershot, leaving 7.25 a.m., arriving Southampton 9.45 a.m.

Battery embarks on three different boats, vehicles in one, horses in another, and personnel not required for these in a third, the *Empress Queen*.

8 p.m. Held up in Southampton Water, submarines being present in Channel.

MAY 21. Boats remain at anchor all day, leaving finally at dusk.

WAR DIARY

May 22. Arrive Havre 12.30 a.m.

Disembarking horses commences from the *Archimedes* at 8 a.m. and continues most of the day. Vehicles also unshipped.

Battery marches to "Point 6" near railway, where it remains for the night.

May 23. Battery entrains during morning, and leaves at 1 p.m. All day spent in train—viâ Rouen.

Water and feed at Montemalier-Buchy.

May 24. Still in train, passing through Abbeville, Boulogne, Calais, arriving St. Omer 1 p.m.

Detraining finishes 5 p.m.

March to Bleue-Maison, 1½ miles west by southwest of Watten, into billets.

May 25. All day at Bleue-Maison.

May 26. All day at Bleue-Maison.

May 27. Leave 12.30 p.m. for Oost-Houck, 7½ miles north-east of St. Omer, arriving 3 p.m.

May 28. Leave 6.30 a.m. for Rouge-Croix, 6 miles west of Bailleul. One gun side-slips into ditch during march, pulling horses in with it. Arrive at destination 1 p.m. Ditched gun arrives 4.15 p.m.

May 29. All day at Rouge-Croix.

May 30. Half Battery personnel (excluding drivers) go to 109 Heavy Battery's position (Major Cobb), near Dranoutre, for three days' instruction, visiting O.P.'s on Mont Kemmel, etc., during the stay;

also position of 115 H.B. north of Neuve-Eglise (Major McAlpine-Leny).

MAY 31. Battery moves to Westoutre, 10 miles south-west of Ypres.

June, 1915

JUNE 1. At Westoutre.

JUNE 2. Other half of Battery to 109 H.B. First half returns.

JUNE 3. At Westoutre. Battery detached from 14th Division about this time.

JUNE 4. At Westoutre.

JUNE 5. At Westoutre. 2nd Lieut. Eastwick-Field evacuated, sick.

JUNE 6. Party from Battery visits 110 Heavy Battery, south of Mont Kemmel.

JUNE 7. Route march during day, orders to be prepared to move in the evening.

JUNE 8. Move 6 p.m., arrive Vert-Route 8.30 p.m., near Bailleul station.

JUNE 9. Move 7.30 p.m. and get into action at Clef-de-Hollande (Le Bizet) near Armentiéres. Horse lines at Pont-de-Nieppe—under 16th Brigade R.G.A. (Lieut.-Colonel Palmer).

JUNE 10. All day preparing position, mapping out A.P.'s, night lines, etc., and selecting O.P.'s, one being on Hill 63, on the edge of Ploegsteert Wood, and the other being the church spire in Le-Bizet (France). A third O.P. was also selected in Le Touquet.

JUNE 11. First round fired from No. 1 gun at 10 a.m. Registering throughout day.

JUNE 12, 13. Registration shoots.

JUNE 14, 15. Registration shoots.

JUNE 16. Battery fired at for first time. One 105 mm. shell lands 30 yards in front—during aeroplane shoot (the first).

JUNE 19. Warwick Heavy Battery on our left shelled out.

JUNE 26. Orders to knock down the Temternrie chimney in Frelinghien. Three observers out. Direct hit in centre; chimney falling down during night.

JUNE 27–30. Various shoots with aero and ground observation on billets and batteries.

2nd Lieut. J. V. Wischer arrives on the 30th.

July, 1915

JULY 3. 2nd Lieut. W. S. A. Jones arrives.

JULY 4–12. Nothing of importance beyond the usual shooting, about thirty rounds per day. A disused position 400 yards in front drew fire intended for us on several occasions.

JULY 13. Raid on enemy trenches 9 p.m., after two mines were exploded. Lively firing for half an hour.

JULY 15. 8-inch how. (the first in action on the front) fires.

JULY 24. Assist 114 Heavy Battery (Major Poole) in a shoot on Messines (9.30 p.m.).

JULY 31. 6.30 p.m., General bombardment by 12th Division, assisted on the right by the 50th Division. Engaged throughout for neutralization, one aeroplane being attached to shoot battery. No infantry attack followed.

During this month wagons were out at 4 a.m. each morning to collect green brushwood to cover battery position.

August, 1915

AUG. 6. 2nd Lieut. Moody arrives (posted from 9 Heavy Battery). 2nd Lieut. Jones leaves to be orderly officer to Brigade.

AUG. 9. Following upon operations around St.' Eloi (Ypres) by the British, the Germans at 3.30 a.m. violently bombarded the whole front from Armentiéres to Messines. Battery was heavily engaged, some 100 rounds being fired, most of which had to be dispatched quickly from wagon lines.

During this month the usual brushwood fatigues went on.

Each day wagons and party went to various places,

such at Neuve Eglise, Chapel d'Armentiéres, Ploegsteert, to collect bricks for the making of horse standings.

Once each week a party went to the Forêt de Nieppe, some 12 miles behind, to fell timber for the construction of the standings.

Standings for 150 horses were finished about the end of the month.

September, 1915

SEPT. 4. Right Section (Captain Wilson, Lieut. Studd, 2nd Lieut. Ward) and 2nd Lieut. Wischer moves to Bac St. Maur, south of Armentiéres, and goes into action following morning—1st Army area.

Left Section (Major Thomas, 2nd Lieut. Young, 2nd Lieut. Moody) remains in position at Le Bizet as Headquarter section.

SEPT. 14–21. Various shoots on trenches in front of Messines, important points in Frelinghien, Warneton, Deulemont, Les Ecluses, took place during this time.

2nd Lieut. Ward posted to 114 Heavy Battery about this time. Right section also fired a lot around Fromelles.

SEPT. 22. Heavy bombardment begins, both sections heavily engaged.

SEPT. 23–24. Bombardment continues.

SEPT. 25. Infantry demonstration and attack in front of Fromelles, without gaining ground.

Strong demonstration between Messines and Armentiéres, but no infantry attack, smoke and gas being used.

Battle of Loos further south, and French offensive in Champagne.

SEPT. 26–31. Activity by the British went on in areas of right and left sections; but in both sectors the reply of the German artillery was very feeble, giving the impression that they were reserving all the ammunition they could.

October, 1915

OCT. 1–12. Very quiet indeed in both sections. All ammunition was now obviously being transferred to the Loos sector.

OCT. 14. Right section returns into position beside left section.

The remainder of the month continued to be very quiet.

OCT. 28. Orders received to be ready to move.

November, 1915

Nov. 1. Battery moves *viâ* Steenwercke, Bailleul, and billets just outside Hazebrouck. 114 and 9 accompany. (2nd Canadian Heavy Battery takes over positions of 14 and 9, one section in each.)

Nov. 2. Move on *viâ* Lillers to billets at Lespesses, 3 miles west of Lillers. Continuous rain throughout day.

Nov. 3. Move *viâ* Pernes and St. Pol to billets at Nuncq. Long march, roughly 25 miles.

Nov. 4. Move *viâ* Frevent to Doullens. Horses were picketed on the high ground beside the citadel, guns being left in the town. Officers and men were billeted in the town.

Nov. 5. Move to Gaudiempre with 9 H.B. (*viâ* Pommera and Mondicourt).

Nov. 6. Battery position selected at Bienvillers-au-Bois (originally French howitzer position, but later occupied by two guns of 19 Heavy Battery (Captain Caldecott)).

Nov. 7–8. Preparing emplacements.

Nov. 9. Preparing emplacements.

Nov. 10. Guns in action. First registration on Le Hameau farm, observing from L.C. (Berles-au-Bois).

Nov. 11–30. Everything was very quiet. The French were on the immediate left, and did no firing whatever.

Horse lines got into very bad condition, horses being entirely in the open.

December, 1915

Dec. 1–10. Fatigue parties to fetch bricks from Rullecourt and Mondicourt. Fairly good brick standings were completed, gunners being brought from Battery.

Dec. 4. Shelled out of one O.P. (L.C.), select another close by. 2nd Lieut. Irvine joins.

Dec. 12. Captain Wilson leaves for England. 1/1 Kent Battery joins the Brigade from England.

Dec. 24. 2nd Lieut. D. Brice joins.

Dec. 25. Christmas passed off well. French on left fraternized with the Germans, and officers and men from both sides were often in no-man's-land during day.

British troops had strict orders not to fraternize.

Dec. 26. Bombardment in enfilade of German trenches facing the French by all four guns. About eighty rounds fired, causing Germans to evacuate their front line at this part and run across open to shelter. French Field Battery assisted latterly.

Dec. 27. Major Thomas leaves for England. Captain Studd temporarily in command.

Dec. 31. Officers at this date as follows :—
Captain Studd, 2nd Lieut. Young, 2nd Lieut. Moody, 2nd Lieut. Wischer, 2nd Lieut. Irvine and 2nd Lieut. Brice.

January, 1916

JAN. 3. Due to shortage of 4·7 ammunition, two of the Battery guns taken out of action to the wagon-lines and two guns of 114 Heavy Battery, under 2nd Lieut. Bagnall, lent to the Battery (60-pounders).

JAN. 10. 1/1 Lowland Battery join the Brigade from England and go into action near Berles-au-Bois.

JAN. 11–23. Fair amount of firing by 60-pounders. Both guns gave trouble by choking from time to time. Targets: Douchy, Adinfer, Hendecourt, and hostile batteries.

JAN. 24. Captain P. S. Wiltshire posted to take command of battery.
    Officers as follows :—
      Right Section: 2nd Lieut. Wischer.
      Left Section: Lieut. Moody.
      B.C. Staff: Lieut. Young.
      A.C.: 2nd Lieut. Brice.

February, 1916

FEB. 1–11. 4·7 guns still out of action—ammunition understood to be going to the guns now being mounted on the ships of the Mercantile Marine.

60-pounders still firing thirty to forty rounds per day, being the only heavy guns in action on the front.

FEB. 12. 2nd Lieut. Sloane-Stanley joins.

FEB. 25. 60-pounders return to 114 on arrival of a limited amount of 4·7 ammunition.

FEB. 27. 2nd Lieut. Wischer seconded to R.F.C.

March, 1916

MAR. 4. Lieut. Moody evacuated, sick.

MAR. 25. 2nd Lieut. Sloane-Stanley to Group as Orderly Officer.

Covered in standings, corrugated on top, canvas round sides, mostly completed this month.

Very little firing beyond area, village, and Battery shoots took place. Fair amount of shooting by aeroplane observation.

April, 1916

APRIL 15. Lieut. Mullis joins from 9 H.B. about this date. 2nd Lieut. Irvine to 9 H.B. in place of Lieut. Mullis.

APRIL. This month, as far as firing went, was fairly uneventful, aeroplane shoots on hostile batteries being the principal work done.

May, 1916

MAY 10. 2nd Lieut. Crouch (formerly Sergeant with 48 H.B.) joins on being commissioned.

MAY 15. 2nd Lieut. C. R. Hodgkinson joins about this time from 114 Heavy Battery, also 2nd Lieut. Sanders from England.

48th Group take over from 16th Group, transferred further south.

MAY 19. Gunner A. M. Everett, B.C. Staff in Bienvillers-au-Bois, during some heavy shelling in which one R.F.A. driver was killed and one wounded badly, one arm being almost severed, carried the latter to a place of safety. For this action, in which he showed the greatest coolness and contempt of danger, he was later awarded the M.M., being the first honour awarded to any one in the Battery.

MAY 25. Orders to be ready to move.

MAY 27. 133 Heavy Battery prepare to take over guns and position from us, with communications, O.P's., etc.

MAY 28. 2nd Lieut. Crouch posted to 133 Heavy Battery.

June, 1916

JUNE 1. Battery hands over guns and vehicles to 133 H.B. and moves to Authieule, near Doullens, to be re-equipped with 60-pounders, brought out by 133 Heavy Battery.

Officers at this time:—
Captain P. S. Wiltshire.
Captain W. J. O. Studd.
Lieut. Mullis: Right Section.
Lieut. Young: B.C. Staff.
2nd Lieut. C. R. Hodgkinson: Left Section.
2nd Lieut. D. Brice: A.C.
2nd Lieut. P. D. Sanders: B.C. Staff.

JUNE 2–6. Taking over and checking equipment, etc., at Authieule.

JUNE 7. Leave 8.30 p.m., travelling *via* Marieux, Louvencourt and Hedauville to Senlis.

JUNE 8. Arrive Senlis 2.30 p.m.

JUNE 9. Battery position selected in front of Martinsart; join 2nd H.A.G. (Col. Massie)—10th Corps.

Group consisting of 14, 24, 108, 114, 122 and 1/1 West Riding H.B. Among the Siege Batteries in the corps were 13, 20, 27, 62 and 80.

WAR DIARY

JUNE 10–14. O.P.'s reconnoitred. Hard at work preparing Battery position.

JUNE 15–23. Guns brought into position and registration carried out on Bois d'Hollande (on the right bank of the Ancre).

O.P.'s one on the ridge north of Mesnil, the other on the spur facing Ovillers. Group O.P. (336) on hill behind Aveluy.

Registration of wire to be cut near Moquet Farm and of communication trenches situated north of Thiepval.

JUNE 24. Big bombardment commences. Wire cutting all day. 2nd Lieut. Sanders wounded at O.P. 19.

Bombr. Muir and Gnr. Adams carried Lieut. Sanders across the open from the front line to the dressing station, for which act of gallantry both were later awarded the M.M.

JUNE 25–29–30. Wire cutting continued, observed during day, and fire maintained at short intervals throughout the night.

Wire also cut with ground observation near Thiepval crucifix.

On latter date bombardments to test barrage, accuracy of fire, etc., were carried out by all Corps Artillery.

Lieut. J. F. Young mentioned in dispatches during month.

July, 1916

July 1. General attack by British and French armies north and south of the Somme.

Attack launched on Corps front at 6.30 a.m. 36th (Ulster) Division penetrated to the outskirts of Grandcourt, capturing Schwaben Redoubt, north of Thiepval.

32nd Division held up in front of Thiepval.

Further north, 4th Division took Serre but had to come back, as 29th Division were held up in front of Beaumont-Hamel.

Further south, 8th Division attacked Ovillers without much success, while 34th Division penetrated into part of La Boiselle.

Further south still the attack was effective, Fricourt and Mametz falling.

The non-success of the 29th and 32nd Divisions compelled the 36th Division to retire to the German support line, which they held.

French were successful south of the river.

July 2. Very heavy German barrage on Thiepval Wood, hampering the communications of the 36th Division.

July 3. On the night of the 3rd, communication trenches were constructed across No-Man's-Land by above Division. La Boiselle taken and front trenches facing Ovillers.

CAPT. E. W. SPALDING, M.C.

WAR DIARY

July 4–6. Firing continued heavily, but on Corps front fighting slackened. 3rd Corps on right still continued heavily.

July 7. Capture of Contalmaison.
2nd Lieut. Spalding joins.

July 8. Loss of Contalmaison, but regained later—on 9th. Retiral to own front line north of Thiepval.

July 9. Casualties in Battery. Battery was shelled consistently during the nights since the 1st, without causing any casualties.

About the 6th there was a blow back, due to a defective tube on No. 3 gun, setting fire to cartridges in the emplacement. Sergt. Keene and some gunners seriously burned. Corpl. Holness at personal risk rescued one of these men while ammunition was still burning, for which he was afterwards awarded the M.M. Sergt. Keene afterwards died of his burns.

July 10–11. Reconnaissances in captured territory as far as Contalmaison Villa, for O.P.'s not successful for Battery purposes.

July 13. Battery ordered to move to Fricourt—cancelled later.

July 14. Capture of Bazentin-le-Petit, Bazentin-le-Grand and Longueval.

Previous fortnight had been a very strenuous one for all personnel in Battery. Battery latterly was firing extreme right in support of the 3rd Corps.
2nd Corps staff relieved 10th Corps.

July 16. Surrender of garrison of Ovillers about this time.
July 20. Battery takes up new position near Aveluy.
July 23. O.P. selected on hill facing Pozieres.
July 24. Capture of Pozieres.
July 25–31. Time spent making O.P.'s, and consolidating generally.

August, 1916

Aug. 1. Fighting became heavy around Moquet Farm.

Aug. 3, 4. Australian and British troops do well round Moquet.

Aug. 5–14. Heavy fighting continued for trenches between Thiepval and Pozieres, and especially round Moquet.

Aug. 15–26. Fighting for and capture of trenches south of Thiepval.
Captain W. J. O. Studd evacuated, sick.

Aug. 27–29. Fighting still round Moquet and Thiepval.

Aug. 30–31. Wire cutting by Battery on front trenches north of Thiepval; observation from O.P. at Mesnil château.

During this month the fighting between Thiepval—Moquet—Pozieres was extremely heavy, and trenches changed hands several times in some cases.

September, 1916

SEPT. 1–2. Wire cutting continued on front line trenches north of Thiepval—successful.

SEPT. 3. 5.10 a.m. Grand assault on whole front—capture of Guillemont and part of Ginchy.

Demonstration astride the Ancre. Got into front trenches, but afterwards compelled to retire to own lines.

SEPT. 4–13. Heavy "crumping" along front.

SEPT. 14. Trenches registered near Leipzig salient; observing from captured trenches near there.

SEPT. 15. Big British attack, using Tanks for first time. Courcelette, Martinpuich, Flers all taken.

Battery fired heavily on trenches registered previous day.

SEPT. 16–21. Attempts to retake lost ground easily repulsed. Continued "crumping."

SEPT. 22–25. Wire cutting on Zollern trench near Thiepval, observing from old German front line at Ovillers.

Successful in every way.

SEPT. 26. 12.35 p.m. Infantry assault on a wide front. Capture of Thiepval.

SEPT. 28. 1 p.m. Thiepval crucifix taken, also Schwaben Redoubt.

SEPT. 29. Battery preparing to move to position near Pozieres.

SEPT. 30. Working party, under Lieut. Mullis, goes to prepare new position. Lieut. Mullis killed by shell fire.

New section, detached from 172 Heavy Battery, arrives, under 2nd Lieut. Dennison, about end of month, to make Battery up to new establishment of six guns.

October, 1916

OCT. 2. Lieut. C. Pearson posted from 122 Heavy Battery.

OCT. 5. Position behind Pozieres nearing completion. Communications laid.

OCT. 6. Left section moves into new position. In action at night, right section firing from old position.

OCT. 7. No. 3 and No. 4 guns calibrated. Destructive shoot on hostile Battery.

OCT. 8. No. 1 and No. 2 guns calibrated in new position.

OCT. 9. New (left) section arrives and goes into action.

OCT. 10. O.P.'s fixed.

OCT. 11. Two new guns calibrated.

OCT. 15. O.P. changed to place immediately in front of Battery (R 34 central—map location).

OCT. 18. Wire cutting at Stuff Redoubt during afternoon.

For the remainder of this month the Battery was always busily engaged, especially on night firing, 50 to 150 rounds on an average per night being fired.

November, 1916

Nov. 2. Three guns condemned and taken to Belle-Eglise to be changed. Due to bad condition of ground, they had to be drawn out of position to road, a distance of nearly 300 yards, by tractor.

Nov. 5. Specially interesting shoot on this date on a Battery situated in front of Loupart Wood—this Battery was barraging on the 3rd Corps front on the right. One gun pit blown up and Battery prevented from taking any further part in the engagement.

Nov. 9. Battery bombarded by gas shell during night. No casualties as all the rounds fell some 400 yards away, though gas drifted into the Battery.

Nov. 11. Firing on this date in support of 4th Canadian Division about Le Sars.

Nov. 14. Capture of Beaumont-Hamel and Hansa Line, 5.45 a.m. Battery barraging River Trench during engagement.

Nov. 15. Battery heavily shelled with 5.9 (H.E. and lachrymatory). One shell penetrated into the B.C. Post, wounding and gassing 2nd Lieut. Dennison and the telephonist.

Nov. 16–27. Usual amount of shelling.

Nov. 28. Reconnoitre near Moquet Farm for new position—unable to find road communications thereto.

December, 1916

Dec. 12. Captain P. S. Wiltshire leaves for England about this date. Captain C. Pearson takes over command.

Very bad weather conditions prevailed during the month, and though night firing was still maintained to harass the Germans, infantry actions were fewer.

THE REMAINING N.C.O.'S AND MEN OF THE ORIGINAL BATTERY WHICH LANDED IN FRANCE, MAY, 1915.
Photo taken in February, 1919, whilst stationed at Neiderzier, Germany.

To face page 45.

January, 1917

JAN. 5. Battery receives orders to be prepared to move.

JAN. 6–7. Preparations for the move.

JAN. 8. 11 p.m. All six guns drawn out of position on to road by tractors.

JAN. 9. 9 a.m. Leave Ovillers.

11.45 a.m. Arrive Senlis.

Difficulty was experienced at wagon-lines in getting clear. The full echelon of ammunition had to be drawn from dump during the previous night, and men and horses were tired.

3 p.m. Leave Senlis. Horses were unable to draw guns up hill at Louvencourt, and motor lorries had to be requisitioned to assist.

After this journey was done very slowly, horses being watered at Marieux.

The vehicles which the horses were able to pull without any great difficulty were collected and pushed on to destination at Warlincourt, arriving there 11.45 p.m.

The remainder of the Battery under 2nd Lieut. Brice remained to cover the journey more slowly, and all except one gun arrived about 3 a.m. next morning.

Remaining gun was left with a guard and brought along by a fresh team next day.

JAN. 10. Orders were issued to proceed to Lattre-St. Quentin, but were impossible to carry out. Notification was sent to 6th Corps H.A. through the 7th Corps to this effect.

JAN. 11. 7.45 a.m. Battery leaves for Lattre-St. Quentin, arriving there at 1.15 p.m.—comes under 47th H.A.G. (Lieut.-Colonel Rumbold).

JAN. 14. Captain C. Pearson returns and resumes command.

JAN. 16. Go to Faubourg d'Amiens (Arras) to select gun position and billets.

During remainder of month guns were not in action, but gunners dug position and assisted in digging others.

February, 1917

FEB. 3. Horse-lines moved to covered standings at Wanquetin, near railhead.

FEB. 11. Horse-lines moved into standings in the village formerly occupied by J Battery R.H.A.

During February the Battery did only a small amount of shooting. This was chiefly for registration and calibration and in response to S.O.S. calls or in support of raids. The gunners were employed in digging our own position in Faubourg d'Amiens and in constructing pits, ammunition recesses and dugouts for several 60-pounder and 6 in. Howitzer Batteries.

FEB. 27. Two guns brought up from wagon-lines to position in Faubourg d'Amiens.

FEB. 28. Four guns (making six in all) in position in Faubourg d'Amiens.

March, 1917

In March the gunners of the Battery continued with the improvement of our own position, including unloading and storing a large reserve of ammunition. They were also employed completing positions for other Batteries and in storing ammunition for them.

Group O.P.'s were manned regularly during the month, but shooting was chiefly confined to registration and in support of raids or in response to S.O.S. signals.

April, 1917

APRIL 1–7. Heavy fighting all along the front.

APRIL 8. In expectation of push, wagon-lines move from Wanquetin to Dainville Wood.

APRIL 9. Attack at dawn; entirely successful, line being pushed forward a minimum of 3½ miles. Battery gets ready to move forward. Position chosen in Faubourg-St. Sauveur and ammunition taken thereto.

Battery actually comes into action behind old front line in Faubourg-St. Sauveur, and is heavily in action at dawn next morning.

APRIL 10. Attack and capture of Monchy-le-Preux. Battery in action all day. Wagon-lines move into old Battery position at Faubourg d'Amiens.

APRIL 11. Battery moves forward and occupies position on Cambrai road. Wagon-lines move in front of Arras, ammunition column remaining at old Battery position.

APRIL 12–18. In support of 3rd Division, and afterwards 15th Division, Battery was very busy, firing as many as 1,800 rounds per day. On latter date five casualties at Battery, shell falling between two of the guns, and on same afternoon three more casualties.

APRIL 20. Two more casualties in Battery.

APRIL 26. Ammunition dump set alight by shell near horse-lines at Faubourg-St. Sauveur. Horses were got away without serious casualty and sent to A.C. at Faubourg d'Amiens.

APRIL 30. Battery moved from Cambrai road position to position behind Wancourt Cemetery. Big number of gas shells taken into position.

May, 1917

May 3. Big attack all along front. Major Pearson wounded during night. Captain Young temporarily in command.

May 5. 2nd Lieut. Brice evacuated, sick.

May 6. Captain R. A. Watson from 35 Heavy Battery takes over command.

May 6–21. Battery in action near Wancourt. A large amount of shooting was done, and the gun position was frequently shelled both by day and night, several casualties resulting. During this period, half the gunners at a time were given four days' rest, which was spent in and about Arras.

May 22. The Battery position was moved from Wancourt to more open country near Feuchy Chapelle behind Monchy. The guns were all withdrawn by 6.30 p.m. and brought into action the same night without any casualties. The wagon-lines remaining in Faubourg-St. Sauveur, Arras.

May 23–31. Battery in action near Feuchy Chapelle. This proved to be an excellent position. The Battery, being well concealed, was not shelled to any extent. A good O.P. was established on Orange Hill and much observed shooting was carried on with good effect, especially on the Drocourt—Queant line, then being constructed by the enemy.

June, 1917

JUNE 1–17. In position at Feuchy Chapelle; much observed shooting was done, and the Battery often fired in support of local attacks round Monchy and Greenland Hill.

JUNE 18. Battery having been ordered to join 1st Army, the guns were pulled out and position vacated at 5 p.m. The Battery assembled at wagon-lines and then marched through Arras to Agnez-Duisans, where they arrived soon after midnight.

JUNE 19–20. Battery rested at Agnez-Duisans. It was now attached to the 13th Corps and was in the 34th H.A.G. commanded by Lieut.-Colonel Liston Fowlis, R.M.A.

JUNE 21. Battery marched to Anzin St. Aubin, where wagon-lines were established.

JUNE 22. Gunners proceed to Battery position near Pt. du Jour to prepare gun-pits. Guns were brought up during the evening and came into action at 9 p.m.

JUNE 23. An O.P. was established near Bailleul behind Oppy—all guns registered.

JUNE 24–30. Very little shooting was done by Battery in this position, the principal work being to stand by for S.O.S. and to fire in support of the attack on Oppy at 7.10 p.m. on the 28th. This attack was completely successful and many prisoners were taken.

July, 1917

JULY 3–7. Battery remained at Anzin St. Aubin, where they were inspected by G.O.C. 13th Corps H.A., who remarked on the fitness of the men.

JULY 8. Right section entrained from Maroeuil for Adinkerke and marched from there through La Panne to Coxyde, where the wagon-lines were established just outside and north-east of the town.

JULY 9. Remainder of Battery entrained from Maroeuil for Dunkerque and marched from there to Coxyde, arriving evening of 10th.

JULY 10. Enemy attacked under cover of intense bombardment, which lasted all day and included all roads and towns in back areas; the attack succeeding in forcing the British line back from the right bank to the left bank of the Yser from Nieuport to the sea.

On this day Lieut. Bishop met the Group Commander (Lieut.-Colonel Liston-Fowlis, R.M.A.), who showed him the Battery position, situated in a small farm in front of Oost Dunkerke on the right of the Oost Dunkerke-Middlekerke Road, and being prepared by some infantry detachment.

The Battery position was behind a small sandbank, and the trees growing along the bank afforded good cover from aircraft observation; but it was impossible to obtain flash cover anywhere owing to the flatness of the country.

JULY 11. Work on Battery position was continued by the gunners.

JULY 12. Platforms for the guns and shell recesses completed, five guns took up the position in the evening. One gun was kept in reserve.

August, 1917

During this month the Battery continued in position in front of Oost Dunkerke. A large amount of shooting was done both by day and night. During the day all shoots were cross observed from the Battery O.P.'s in Nieuport and Nieuport Bains respectively.

Although the Battery was not subjected to any destructive shoots, the personnel were considerably harassed both by day and night by hostile shelling of the Battery and roads and light railways close by.

Several casualties occurred, including 2nd Lieut. **A. W. B.** Peggie and 2nd Lieut. P. Purdie, both killed on the night of 17/18th.

September, 1917

SEPT. 2. Battery transferred to 1st H.A.G., under command of Lieut.-Colonel Lockhart, R.G.A.

SECOND LIEUT. A. W. B. PEGGIE.
Killed in action, August 17, 1917.

To face page 52.

SEPT. 5. The wagon-lines at Coxyde were bombed by enemy aircraft on the night 5/6th, one man killed and four wounded. The following day wagon-lines moved to Bray Dunes, only the officers' chargers being left at forward wagon-lines between Coxyde and La Panne.

During the month the Battery continued to be very active, and cross observation was carried out as in August. Harassing fire by the enemy continued, and several casualties occurred.

October, 1917

OCT. 9. The Battery was subjected to a destructive shoot, about 300 15-cm. shells falling in and around position between 10.45 a.m. and 1.40 p.m.—one man killed and one wounded. No casualties to guns, although a few cartridges were destroyed.

Battery firing with cross observation was continued, and enemy shelling at frequent intervals caused a few casualties, but no damage to equipment.

November, 1917

Lieut.-Colonel Langhorne took command of 1st H.A.G. in place of Lieut.-Colonel Lockhart invalided to England.

Nov. 10. Major R. A. Watson, M.C., proceeded to England on B.C.'s course.

Nov. 11. Battery again subjected to a destructive shoot, but by courageous action of 2nd Lieut. C. H. Scott and Sergt. Jackson in putting up a smoke screen before ranging was completed no casualties occurred, and the only material damage was one gun wheel slightly damaged.

For this work 2nd Lieut. C. H. Scott was awarded the M.C. and Sergt. S. Jackson the M.M. About 300 rounds of 15-cm. were fired at Battery.

Battery activity continued, but less shooting was undertaken than in the previous months.

December, 1917

Dec. 1–3. In action in front of Oost-Dunkerke.

Dec. 4. Position taken over by the French. Battery moved to wagon-lines on the evening of 4th.

The night of 4th/5th was spent at the wagon-lines at Bray Dunes. Hostile aircraft dropped bombs on the vehicles at night, and one limbered wagon was damaged and some cartridges destroyed.

Dec. 5. Battery moved from Bray Dunes at 6.30 a.m. and travelled by road to Wormhoult, where the men were billeted in a barn for the night.

Dec. 6. Battery moved off at 6 a.m. and proceeded to Buysscheure. Men were billeted in barns, and the horse-lines were in an open field without standings.

Dec. 7–26. Battery engaged in training. Sports were organized in conjunction with other Heavy Batteries (140 H.B., 127 H.B. and 138 H.B.) resting in the neighbourhood.

Dec. 26. Battery ordered to move to Therouanne to join the 92nd Heavy Artillery Brigade. Unable to move owing to severe frost and snow.

Dec. 26–31. Training at Buysscheure continued.

January, 1918

JAN. 1–10. Training at Buysscheure continued.

The Battery was unable to move owing to the snow and frosty state of the roads.

JAN. 11. Battery moved off at 9 a.m., and proceeded by road to Crecques, where it arrived at 7.30 p.m. Officers and men accommodated in billets. Horses picketed along a side road.

JAN. 12. Battery rested at Crecques.

JAN. 13. Battery left at 9.45 a.m. and proceeded to Ecquedecques, arriving at 2.30 p.m.

JAN. 14. Battery rested at Ecquedecques.

JAN. 15. Battery left at 8.30 a.m. and proceeded to Hersin-Coupigny, arriving at 3.30 p.m.

JAN. 16–31. Battery in training at Hersin.

The 92nd Bde. was commanded by Lieut.-Colonel F. E. Courtney, D.S.O., and consisted of the following Batteries:—

14 Heavy Battery R.G.A.
127 Heavy Battery R.G.A.
129 Heavy Battery R.G.A.
1/1 Kents Heavy Battery R.G.A.

The Brigade was attached to Canadian Corps for Administration, but for fighting formed part of G.H.Q. reserve.

February, 1918

During February the Battery continued training at Hersin.

A reserve position was prepared on the Vimy Ridge.

March, 1918

MAR. 1–21. Battery continued training at Hersin.

MAR. 21. Brigade received orders to be prepared to move at a moment's notice. All vehicles were packed and preparations for the march completed.

MAR. 22. Battery moved off from Hersin at 9.30 a.m., and marched *via* Villers-au-Bois and Warlus to Wanquetin, arriving at 7 p.m. The whole Brigade were billeted together in Nisson huts.

MAR. 23. The Brigade moved off in the following order: 14 H.B., 129 H.B., 127 H.B. and 1/1 Kents at 5 a.m. and marched to Bucquoy, where the head of the column halted in the village and horses were watered and fed.

The Brigade moved on again at 6 p.m. and 14 H.B. came into position near Achiet-le-Grand, and all guns were in action by 10 p.m.

Wagon-lines were established at Achiet-le-Petit.

MAR. 24. Battery opened fire on Vaulx at 5 a.m., and fired at intervals during the day. At 5.30 p.m. orders were received to retire to the site of the wagon-lines in front of Achiet-le-Petit, and the guns were promptly got into position there. Later a further retirement was ordered, and the night was spent on the road in Bucquoy.

MAR. 25. Battery came into action behind Bucquoy at 10 a.m., the wagon-lines being in front of Essarts; about 50 rounds were fired on Bapaume. At 12.30 p.m. the Battery retired *viâ* Hannescamp to a position between Fonquevillers and Sailly-au-Bois, but did not fire.

MAR. 26. At 5 a.m. the Battery advanced again to near its old position behind Bucquoy, but, owing to the tactical situation, did not come into action, but returned to its position of the previous night. Almost immediately it arrived there, owing to the rapid advance of the enemy, it was ordered to retire, and eventually came into action at Souastre Fork, on the road between Fonquevillers and Souastre. Wagon-lines were established just in front of Souastre. The first position taken up in this neighbourhood was in the open, with the object of being able to fire on the enemy with open sights in case they came over the crest at Hebuterne. They did not get as far, as the New Zealand Division, and the 4th Australian Infantry Brigade came up and counter-attacked, saving the situation. Two days later the guns were moved back about 100 yards in order to get flash cover behind the crest. Soon after coming into this position an enemy aeroplane swooped down and fired on the Battery with its machine gun, but did not inflict any casualties. The aeroplane was shot down by rifle fire.

April, 1918

During April the Battery continued in position at Souastre Fork between Fonquevillers and Souastre. The wagon-lines were just outside Souastre.

A large amount of shooting was done both by day and night. A Brigade O.P. was established near the Crucifix at Hebuterne, which was manned every day by 14 H.B. and every night by all the Batteries in the Brigade in turn. This O.P. was in communication with the Infantry Brigade and with the Battery by both telephone and visual. On clear days the Brigade frequently fired on movement around Puiseux and the roads further east, and every night harassing fire was kept up on roads and tracks, railways, and communication trenches. The Battery was also frequently called upon to neutralize hostile batteries.

AEROPLANE PHOTOGRAPH OF BATTERY POSITION, SOUASTRE. FORK. APRIL, 1918.

The gun pits can be seen above the arrow. No camouflage was attempted.

To face page 60.

APRIL 5. The Battery was heavily shelled with 15 cm., 10·5 cm. and 77 mm. from 5 a.m. till about 9.30 a.m., but continued in action throughout the time. For courage and coolness displayed on this occasion, Cpl. Wootton and Cpl. Holman were awarded the M.M. and 2nd Lieut. Baird awarded M.C.

At intervals during the month the Battery was shelled, and a few slight casualties occurred.

APRIL 7. Acting Captain J. F. Young left the Battery to be second in command of 262 S. Battery. His place was taken by Acting Captain H. H. Hutchinson, M.C., from 127th H. Battery.

May, 1918

MAY 1-10. Battery continued in action near Souastre Fork. A large amount of shooting both by day and night was carried out. A feature of the firing at this time was that it nearly all took place at ranges varying from ten thousand to fourteen thousand yards. The guns and carriages were thus brought under exceptionally severe strain, so that they soon wore out. The Battery was occasionally shelled with 8-inch armour-piercing shells, one of which exploded near No. 2 gun, lifting it bodily and throwing it against the side of the pit without damaging it.

MAY 11. Battery position moved to the Willow Patch A, about 1,500 yards south of Bienvillers. The position was camouflaged and pits prepared. The guns were brought in at dusk and the whole position very carefully concealed, as the Battery was to remain silent until specially ordered to fire. Billets for the men were prepared behind a crest about 400 yards in rear of the guns.

MAY 17–30. The Battery remained silent. The O.P. was manned by day and night, and visual communication established and practised regularly between O.P. and Battery and Battery and Brigade.

MAY 1–30. The wagon-lines were near Souastre, and, being so near the fighting zone, were occasionally troubled by shelling evidently intended for roads and tracks close by. Advantage was taken of the Battery being silent to train drivers and Nos. 1 in riding drill, and under the personal command of the O.C. each evening a riding school, including jumping, was organized. Some very successful riding and jumping was accomplished, much to the benefit of horses and men.

MAY 30. Wagon-lines moved to temporary site near St. Armand.

MAY 31. The Battery pulled out from its silent position at 12.30 a.m. and moved to Hannescamp, taking over the positions vacated by 133 H.B. and 147 H.B. The guns were in action by 4 a.m. Registration was carried out during the morning, and in the afternoon the Battery was shelled by 15 cm. Howitzers. One gun was put out of action by a direct hit on the travelling wheel, and two men were wounded.

On the whole, during the time the Battery was in this position, it was not much troubled by hostile fire. The guns were widely separated and fairly well camouflaged. At a later date, when a copy of a German counter-battery map fell into our hands it was found that they had accurately located all of our guns except one (D sub.). In addition, they had shown the officers' cook-house as a gun position.

June, 1918

During the whole of June the Battery was in action near Hannescamp. The wagon-lines were situated between Henu and Souastre, and the ammunition column was at Sarton. The O.P. was near Gommecourt, and commanded an excellent view.

A large amount of shooting was done both by day and night. Many shoots were observed from the O.P. on movement and hostile batteries, and two shoots with aeroplane observation were carried out very satisfactorily.

On June 30 the Battery took an active part in the IVth Corps H.A. Horse Show, and gained the following prizes :—

    1st Prize: "Wrestling on Horseback."
    2nd Prize: "Tug of War on Horseback."
    2nd Prize: "Alarm Race."
    3rd Prize: "Best turn-out Limbered Wagon and Team."

JUNE 28. Lieut. G. H. Bishop left Battery on promotion to Acting Captain and took over Second in Command of 1/1 Kents Heavy Battery R.G.A.

July, 1918

During July the Battery continued in action near Hannescamp. The wagon-lines were between Henu and Souastre and the O.P. near Gommecourt. The ammunition column remained at Sarton.

Owing to various batteries having left the Corps, the Battery did even more shooting than in June. The condition of the horses continued to improve, and the work of the Battery was in every way satisfactory.

During the month firing was almost continuous. Several bombardments took place in support of raids and Livens projector attacks. Much observed shooting was done on batteries and movement in the neighbourhood of Puisieux, and on transport on Handels Road, and roads running out of Grevillers. Registration and calibration shoots were frequently carried out with the aid of the Field Survey Company, principally on Puisieux Church. In the process the few remaining bricks were soon reduced to dust.

The Battery had a very large counter-battery area, and was constantly busy firing on hostile batteries, sometimes with aeroplane and balloon observation. Later, when it was possible to visit the positions of some of the batteries fired on, it was found that those in the neighbourhood of Puisieux were so knocked about that it was almost impossible to tell where they had been. Others in the Loupart Wood area were not quite so bad, but all had suffered very severely.

August, 1918

AUG. 1–21. Battery in action near Hannescamp. Wagon-lines between Henu and Souastre, and ammunition column at Sarton. The Battery was complimented by the D.D.V.S., 3rd Army, upon its horse mastership and the excellent condition of horses and horse-lines.

AUG. 21. The Battery took a very active part in the advance beginning to-day. Fire was opened at zero hour 4.55 a.m., and continued to 7.47 a.m. bombarding Bihucourt.

At 8 a.m., in accordance with previous orders, the Battery moved forward and came into action near Biez Wood, behind Bucquoy, at 9 a.m. The wagon-lines moved up to the vacated Battery position near Hannescamp, and the ammunition column occupied the old wagon-lines. The O.C. moved up behind the infantry to Logeast Wood, and sent back valuable information as to the situation. The Battery continued to fire on communications and answered a large number of N.F. and G.F. calls. Thirty-three targets were engaged during the day, 1,200 rounds being fired.

Aug. 22. The Battery continued to fire on communications and to answer N.F. and G.F. calls. Twenty-six targets were engaged and 576 rounds fired. During the day three men were seriously wounded in the Battery by shell fire, and the N.C.O. observer at the O.P. was wounded by a machine-gun bullet, and was carried to the dressing station by 2nd Lieut. S. C. Petrie under heavy fire.

Aug. 23. The Battery continued in action behind Bucquoy and fired 954 rounds on twenty-three targets, including N.F. and G.F. calls and the bombardment of communications.

Aug. 24. At dawn the Battery moved forward to a position in front of Achiet-le-Petit, and the O.P. was established on the left of Grevillers overlooking Bapaume. The wagon-lines and the ammunition column moved up to the position vacated by the Battery behind Bucquoy.

It is interesting to note that the positions occupied by the Battery during the advance were in each case approximately those held during the retreat in March, 1918. Satisfaction was felt by the personnel in the fact that the lost ground was thus regained.

Aug. 25. The Battery continued in action near Achiet-le-Petit and fired on enemy communications and hostile batteries in answer to N.F. calls. During the afternoon two men were seriously wounded, by the breech block of a gun being blown out.

Aug. 26. At dawn the Battery moved to position in front of Bihucourt, and the O.P. was established near Loupart Wood.

Aug. 27. The Battery continued in position near Bihucourt. During the evening three men and five horses were wounded in the wagon-lines.

Aug. 28. The Battery remained at Bihucourt, and the O.P. was moved to the front line north of Beugnâtre.

Aug. 29. At 6 p.m. the Battery left Bihucourt and came into action to the east of Biefvillers. During the night sleeping quarters were shelled, but no casualties resulted.

The wagon-lines moved up to Bihucourt.

Aug. 30. At 9 p.m. the Battery moved to position near Favreuil.

Aug. 31. The Battery fired from its position at Favreuil on N.F. and G.F. calls and on enemy communications. At night Battery was bombed, but no damage done. 129 H.B. only a few yards away had five men killed.

Throughout the advance the behaviour of the men had been excellent, in spite of much hard work and very little sleep. In every case the Battery was brought into action smartly and without a hitch, due to the good work of the men and the fine working condition of the horses.

September, 1918.

Sept. 1. Battery at Favreuil, O.P. at Beugnâtre.

Sept. 2. Battery fired in support of an infantry attack on 4th and 6th Corps' front.

Sept. 3. Enemy retired several miles as result of previous day's success. Battery moved to position between Fremicourt and Velu. Wagon-lines moved to near Fremicourt.

Sept. 4. O.P. established near waterworks at Bertincourt; two enemy batteries neutralized by observed fire. About noon Battery moved to position near Velu Wood.

Sept. 5. Considerable fire on battery position by H.V. guns during previous night.

Sept. 6. O.P. moved to Neuville Bourjonval. Enemy during this time being gradually driven back by New Zealanders. Metz and greater part of Havrincourt Wood captured during day.

Sept. 7. Battery position shelled during night by H.V. guns. Cpl. Metcalfe, Gnr. Baker and Chesterman wounded. During all this time the Battery was engaged on harassing fire during nights and in concentrations and N.F. calls during day. At noon Battery moved to position near Ruyaulcourt.

Sept. 8. O.P. established on mound near Metz. Lieut. E. W. Spalding, M.C., promoted to Captain, and took over second in command 103 S. Battery.

Sept. 9. Usual programme of firing carried out. No engagements of importance on our immediate front. Our troops now within a short distance of line from which they retreated in March. Enemy resistance stiffens.

Sept. 10. Battery moved to position between Neuville Bourjonval and Havrincourt Wood. During the first thirty-six hours in this position the Battery fired over 2,000 rounds.

Sept. 11. Artillery fire on both sides very severe. Enemy bombing planes were very active during night. Three were seen to have been brought down during one night.

Sept. 12. O.P. moved to Trig Post on Beaucamp Ridge. This was a very useful O.P., but great difficulty was experienced in maintaining communication with the Battery owing to heavy shell fire. Enemy machine-gunners and snipers were also very active. The work of the telephonists and linesmen was carried out under conditions of exceptional danger.

Sept. 13. Traffic on Gouzeaucourt-Cambrai Road engaged and a considerable number of N.F. calls answered.

Sept. 14. Usual programme carried out, 150 rounds per night being fired in the harassing of roads, etc.

Sept. 15. Most of the firing during this time consisted of three-minute concentrations on targets allotted by Brigade, answers to N.F. and G.F. calls, night harassing fire, and observed shooting on roads and batteries near Gouzeaucourt and Gonnelieu.

Sept. 16. Usual firing. 240 rounds of gas shell were fired on hostile battery positions.

Sept. 17. On account of continued large, daily expenditure of ammunition the horses and drivers, were under a continual heavy strain. Fortunately the hard work appeared to have no bad effect on the horses, and they still maintained their former high state of efficiency.

Sept. 18. At 5.20 a.m. an attack commenced over a wide front. On our immediate front the advance was only a few hundred yards in depth. Battery fired 370 rounds, neutralizing hostile batteries. At 5 p.m. enemy counter-attacked 6th Corps on our left, and succeeded in recapturing the village of Moeuvres.

Sept. 19–21. The usual counter-battery work and harassing fire on roads was carried out. A considerable amount of observed shooting on movement on the Gouzeaucourt-Cambrai Road was done.

Sept. 22. Major R. A. Watson, M.C., went on leave, Captain H. H. Hutchinson, M.C., taking command.

Sept. 23. Usual firing in answer to aeroplane calls, and on movement, and harassing fire on Couillet Valley.

Sept. 24. The quietest day experienced by the Battery since September 8, less than 100 rounds being fired. About this time Captain Hutchinson was forced by illness to return to the wagon-lines at Ytres, leaving the firing battery in command of Lieut. C. H. Scott, M.C.

SEPT. 25. Roads were intermittently harassed during the day and night, and active hostile batteries engaged.

SEPT. 26. A considerable amount of firing on the usual targets was carried out.

SEPT. 27. An attack on a wide front was launched by the British, the attack commencing at varying hours, on our front at 5 a.m. Hostile fire in retaliation was heavy throughout the day, and the linesmen performed excellent service in keeping communication. Sergt. Street was wounded at the Battery position. The attack had limited objectives on our front, and a more forward O.P. could not be established. At midnight the Battery moved to Winchester Valley near Metz, and came under fire from light artillery while occupying the position, Sergt. Dale, M.M., and Gnr. Searson being wounded. During the eighteen days the Battery was at Neuville Bourjonval nearly 7,000 rounds were fired, all of which was brought up by horse transport. A considerable amount of work was done at the wagon-lines at Ytres to provide suitable standings for the horses, which were in excellent condition.

SEPT. 28. Both artilleries were active to-day, though hostile activity on back areas was mainly confined to high velocity guns, otherwise known as "Toute Suiters." The attack was continued to-day.

Sept. 29. Captain Hutchinson had to leave the Battery owing to illness, and Lieut. C. H. Scott, M.C., took command. Much firing on roads and active batteries took place and also on the bridges over the St. Quentin Canal at Masnieres and Banteaux.

Sept. 30. The Battery moved to a position near Gonnelieu, and the wagon-lines were established at Gouzeaucourt.

October, 1918

Oct. 1. O.P. established on Bonavis Spur, commanding an excellent view of part of the Hindenburg Line, and the first view of complete houses in the war zone for many months, providing excellent shooting. It may be mentioned that in spite of competition by the Field Artillery, a 60-pounder was responsible for the first hole in Fox Farm.

Oct. 2. Little shooting was done from the Gonnelieu position. The enemy country was apparently deserted by day, only one shoot on movement being carried out during three days.

Oct. 3. The Battery moved to a position in the Hindenburg Support Line, near the Gouzeaucourt-Cambrai Road. Firing mostly on Briseaux Wood near Lesdain. O.P. moved to neighbourhood of Lateau Wood.

Oct. 4. Heavy firing during day and night on active batteries, twenty-one being engaged, and on Pelu Wood.

Oct. 5. Hostile artillery was again very active, and neutralizing fire was brought to bear on them during the hours of daylight. Night firing took place on Wambaix at a range of over eight miles.

Oct. 6. Battery in position in the Hindenburg Line. Usual firing.

Oct. 7. Battery moved to new position near Banteaux.

Oct. 8. At 4.30 a.m. commenced firing in support of an infantry attack on the Masnieres-Beaurevoir Line. O.P. now near Hurtubise Farm.

At 7 a.m. Battery moved forward to new position near Cheneux Wood. Had difficulty in crossing the St. Quentin Canal. One horse fell in, but was rescued.

Oct. 9. Wagon-lines were moved from Gouzeaucourt to Banteaux. Enemy were retiring, so that Battery was out of range by 9 a.m. We now come under the control of the New Zealand Divisional Artillery. At 3 p.m. Battery moved to position near Esnes. Wagon-lines were established near Lesdains. Harassing fire during night.

Oct. 10. Left section under 2nd Lieut. S. C. Petrie moved forward in morning to position of readiness east of Longsart, and in afternoon went into action near Fontaine-au-Pire. Remainder of Battery moved up during afternoon and came into action west of Beauvois.

OCT. 11. Battery moved up and joined left section at Fontaine-au-Pire, and the whole moved forward with instructions to go into action near Ferme-au-Tertre. Owing to heavy shelling of the road through Quievy it was found impossible to do so, so went into action near Quievy. Considerable difficulty was experienced during these days in getting the guns forward owing to the enemy having blown up all the important bridges and cross-roads during his retreat.

OCT. 12. In action at Quievy. In the last few days the Battery has left the shell-torn country and entered country which is almost undamaged by shell fire. A large number of German military gardens provide a much-needed and much-appreciated supply of vegetables for the men.

OCT. 13-19. Usual harassing fire principally on roads in vicinity of Beaurain and Romeries. O.P. near Ferme-au-Tertre. Misty weather interferes with observed shooting. Wagon-lines at Bevillers. Battery again under tactical control of 92nd Brigade R.G.A. When the Battery left the N.Z.D.A. Lieut.-Colonel McQuarrie, commanding 2nd Brigade N.Z.F.A., spoke very appreciatively of the work of the Battery while under his command.

During the preceding weeks of continuous fighting the supply of signal cable had become exceedingly short, but due largely to the energy and hard work of Cpl. Everett, M.M., N.C.O. i/c of the B.C. staff, the Battery had always been able to maintain its proper communications.

Oct. 20. An attack which succeeded in securing the crossings of the Selle and in capturing Solesmes was undertaken to-day. Battery fired 600 rounds on counter-battery work. Signaller Corbett was severely wounded in the leg. 2nd Lieut. Petrie, M.C., and Bombr. Bingham succeeded in getting him out of the danger zone at considerable risk to themselves. In the afternoon the Battery moved to a position near Ferme-au-Tertre. It was at this place that the left wing of the British Army rested when the 2nd Corps made a stand on August 26, 1914.

Oct. 21. In action at Ferme-au-Tertre.

Oct. 22. Battery crossed the Selle River and came into action near Briastre. Wagon-lines moved to Ferme-au-Tertre. At night, owing to the collapse of a pontoon bridge over the Selle, an ammunition wagon and team fell into the river. Two horses were drowned.

Oct. 23. An attack on a wide front commenced at 2.30 a.m. Battery came under heavy hostile fire by H.V. guns from 3 a.m. to 6 a.m. Fortunately most of the shells fell either over or to the left, and no damage was done. Battery fired over 600 rounds on counter-batteries. A satisfactory feature of this shooting was that the following day we were able to visit the positions of the three targets engaged. In all cases the shooting was almost perfect.

Oct. 24. Battery again comes under the control of the N.Z.D.A. and moves to La Trousse Miñou, east of Romeries. Wagon-lines at Romeries. O.P. south-west of Ferme-au-Bearte. Harassing fire on roads east and north-east of Le Quesnoy.

Oct. 25–31. Battery remains in action at the above position. Again under 92nd Brigade R.G.A. Usual programme of concentrations and harassing fire.

Major R. A. Watson, M.C., returns from leave and takes over command of Battery. During the period of his absence Lieut. C. H. Scott, M.C., had very successfully commanded the Battery through a very trying time.

During the preceding six months Cpl. Bloor, W.A., has very satisfactorily performed the duties of B.C.'s assistant. The thoroughness and unfailing accuracy which marked all his work was much appreciated by all the officers.

During the whole of this month Lieut. Baird and his O.P. party did some excellent forward observation work, which brought considerable credit to the Battery. Lieut. Baird was often mentioned by Battalion Commanders, and eventually was awarded a Bar to the M.C. This officer knew no fear.

November, 1918

Nov. 1. To-day No. 2 gun (B sub-section) had a premature, completely destroying the gun and wounding Cpl. Meehan, Bdr. Lee, Gnrs. Ellis and Edwards—the last battle casualties suffered by the Battery in the War.

Nov. 2. Left section moved to a position near Sepmeries at 4 p.m. Owing to congested roads and steep hills they did not get into action until 3 a.m. on the 3rd. Roads in vicinity of position were under heavy shell fire, but due largely to the skill and courage of Sergt. Harkes the horses were all got away safely.

Nov. 4. At 3.30 a.m. commenced firing on counter-batteries in support of the last large operation on this front. Attack was very successful. Le Quesnoy was surrounded early in the day, but did not surrender until 5 p.m. In the afternoon the Battery moved to Fm. de Ft. Martin, the left section rejoining it late at night.

Nov. 5. Battery moved early in the morning to Villerau, being attached to the New Zealand Divisional Artillery, and commenced firing on the crossings of the River Sambre at Pont-sur-Sambre and Hautmont. During the day the Battery came under control of 42nd Div. Artillery.

Nov. 6. Battery moved at dawn to position in Mormal Forest. In action at 9 a.m. Raining heavily and roads very bad, all important bridges being blown up. This was the last position occupied by the Battery in the War. Battery has now advanced about sixty miles since the commencement of the offensive on August 21.

Nov. 7. Harassing fire on roads continued, 200 rounds being expended. Enemy still retiring.

Nov. 8. Harassing fire on roads east of Hautmont until 10 a.m. From information received it appeared that the enemy was out of range, so "Cease Firing" was ordered at 10 a.m., the last round being fired by No. 2 gun (E sub-section), Sergt. Waddington being the No. 1.

Nov. 9–10. Still in action at same place as no bridges capable of carrying 60-pounders are as yet erected. Wagon-lines at La Grande Carriere.

Nov. 11. The Armistice came into force at 11 a.m. On our front the farthest Cavalry outposts were at Obies and the Farm of Quatre Bras. Enemy were holding Cousolre. The most noticeable feature of the day was the small amount of excitement caused by the announcement of the cessation of hostilities.

    Officers of the Battery now are:—

    Major R. A. Watson, M.C.: Officer Commanding.
    Captain G. H. Bishop: Second in Command.
    Lieut. G. R. Bromley: Right Section.

Lieut. C. H. Scott, M.C.: Centre Section.
2nd Lieut. S. C. Petrie, M.C.: Left Section.
2nd Lieut. W. J. Baird, M.C.: Observation Officer.
2nd Lieut. T. M. Witherow, Ammunition Column.
2nd Lieut. E. Hanson.
2nd Lieut. H. Downes.
2nd Lieut. M. Fitzgerald.
2nd Lieut. Spencer.

During the past three months the Battery has fired 32,269 rounds, representing 880 tons of metal.

Nov. 12. Still at La Grande Carriere, Battery occupying cage formerly occupied by British prisoners of war employed in the Foret de Mormal.

Nov. 13. Battery was inspected by G.O.C. R.A. 4th Corps, and was complimented on the condition of the men, horses and guns.

A copy of a letter written from the G.O.C. 42nd Division to B.G.C.H.A., 4th Corps, in which he spoke very highly of the work of 14 Heavy Battery, was received.

CONFIDENTIAL.   4th Corps H.A. No. 487/79/8.

O.C., 90th Brigade R.G.A.
O.C., 92nd Brigade R.G.A.

The B.G.C.H.A. directs me to send you the attached copy of a letter he has received from the G.O.C., 42nd Division.

The B.G.C.H.A. wishes to add his thanks for the good work done.

(Signed) G. DARBY,
Captain, R.A.

[Copy of letter.]
H.Q., 4th Corps H.A.   Staff Captain, R.A.
    16th November, 1918   4th Corps H.A.

DEAR MARSHALL,—

As the 14th Heavy and the 244th Siege Batteries of the 92nd and 90th Brigades R.G.A. are now leaving the Division under my Command, I should like to let you know how much their good work has been appreciated by all ranks of both Infantry and Field Artillery. The 14th Heavy Battery in particular behaved magnificently in pushing forward their guns in the Foret de Mormal in close support of the Infantry under extremely difficult conditions.

Will you please convey our thanks for all they have done for us to all the officers and men concerned.

Wishing them good luck on the march.

                    Yours Sincerely
                  (Signed) A. SOLLY-FLOOD.

14th November 1918

Nov. 14. Battery moved to rejoin the rest of the 92nd Brigade at Salesches.

Nov. 15–19. At Salesches, refitting and preparing to march to the Rhine.

Nov. 20. Brigade commenced the march, moving off in the following order: 1/1 Kent H.B., 14 H.B., 127 H.B., 129 H.B. Halted at Amfroipret.

Nov. 23. Battery moved to La Grisoelle.

Nov. 25. Battery moved to Binche, the first town seen in which conditions approximated those of peace time.

    The places at which we halted and the dates upon which we moved during the remainder of the march are shown below.

Nov. 28. Binche to Marchiennes-au-Pont.

TAKEN AT BINGHE, BELGIUM, NOVEMBER, 1918, WHILST ON "MARCH TO THE RHINE."

(Standing)—
Lt. T. M. Witherow, Lt. W. J. Baird, M.C., Lt. R. Bromley, 2nd Lt. M. Fitzgerald, Lt. S. Brown, U.S.A., 2nd Lt. E. Hanson, Lt. S. C. Petrie, M.C
(Sitting).—Lt. C. H. Scott, M.C., Major McKenzie, M.C. (129th H.B.), Major R. A. Watson, M.C., Capt. G. H. Bishop, Rev. — Coles.

To face page 80.

December, 1918

Dec. 1. Marchiennes-au-Pont to Chatelet.
Dec. 4. Chatelet to Bois de Villiers.
Dec. 5. Bois de Villiers to Gives.
Dec. 6. Gives to Lives.
Dec. 7. Lives to Viesset Barse.
Dec. 8. Viesset Barse to Xhoris.
Dec. 10. Xhoris to Stoumont.
Dec. 11. Stoumont to Malmedy.
 To-day the Battery crossed the frontier, and entered Germany. Considerable satisfaction was felt by every one at being able, after so many years' endeavour, finally to set foot in Germany as part of a conquering army.
Dec. 12. Malmedy to Weywertz.
Dec. 13. Weywertz to Kalterherburg.
Dec. 14. Kalterherburg to Simmerath.
Dec. 16. Simmerath to Lammersdorf.
Dec. 18. Lammersdorf to Rolsdorf.
Dec. 20. Rolsdorf to Schlich.
Dec. 21–27. Schlich is a rather small, dirty village, but the men were fairly comfortably housed, there being two or three in each house in the village. The

horses were similarly scattered around among the stables of the village.

For Christmas Day the Battery was fortunate in obtaining a supply of fresh pork, vegetables, oranges, nuts, etc., so all ranks had a very good Christmas Dinner. The Dinner was held in the village beir hall, and altogether the day passed very pleasantly.

DEC. 29. Demobilization commenced with the release of some coal-miners.

JAN. 4, 1919. Schlich to Neiderzier.

ROLL OF HONOUR

Casualties to Officers, N.C.O.'s and Men whilst Serving with the Battery

2ND LIEUT. P. D. SANDERS. Wounded, near Ovillers, June 24, 1916.

42144 GNR. J. H. BARRY. Wounded, near Ovillers, June 27, 1916.

28830 SERGT. R. KEENE. Wounded, burns, at Martinsart, July 2, 1916. Died of wounds.

69887 GNR. T. RICHARDSON. Wounded, burns, at Martinsart, July 2, 1916. Died of wounds.

41721 GNR. R. SWIFT. Wounded, burns, at Martinsart, July 2, 1916.

63303 GNR. W. LAWRENCE. Wounded, burns, at Martinsart, July 2, 1916. Died of wounds.

42174 GNR. E. SPELLING. Wounded, burns, at Martinsart, July 2, 1916.

44511 Gnr. D. PREECE. Wounded, burns, at Martinsart, July 2, 1916.

44935 Gnr. R. KEENAN. Wounded, at Martinsart, July 3, 1916.

69420 Gnr. A. EDWARDS. Shell wound, chest, at Martinsart, July 9, 1916.

Lieut. G. E. MULLIS. Killed in action, near Pozieres, September 30, 1916.

70226 Gnr. J. A. SKELDON. Gunshot wounds, near Pozieres, September 30, 1916.

42194 Gnr. A. HARDING. Gunshot wounds, near Pozieres, September 30, 1916.

45056 Gnr. PET. McKEOWN. Gunshot wounds, near Pozieres, September 30, 1916.

42134 Act. Bdr. P. BATES. Gunshot wounds, near Pozieres, September 30, 1916.

59639 Gnr. C. H. BUSHELL. Gunshot wounds, near Pozieres, September 30, 1916.

3630 Gnr. T. D. FORDE. Gunshot wounds, near Pozieres, September 30, 1916.

88199 Gnr. J. L. TAYLOR. Wounded, near Ovillers, October 20, 1916. Died of wounds (buried in Varennes, 6¼ miles north-west of Albert).

2nd Lieut. C. D. DENISON. Wounded and gassed near Ovillers, November 15, 1916.

Gnr. H. BEDFORD. Wounded and gassed, near Ovillers, November 15, 1916.

ROLL OF HONOUR

97441 G<small>NR</small>. BOOTLE. Wounded and gassed, at Faubourg d'Amiens, Arras, April 1917. Died of wounds.

28875 G<small>NR</small>. G. PAISLEY. Wounded, at Faubourg d'Amiens, Arras, April 4, 1917. Died of wounds.

50159 C<small>ORPL</small>. E. G. EEDY. Shell wound, shoulder, on Cambrai Road, near Tilloy, April 18, 1917. To U.K.

42191 A<small>CT</small>. B<small>DR</small>. W. TATE. Shell wound, leg, face and hand, on Cambrai Road, near Tilloy, April 18, 1917. To U.K.

76220 G<small>NR</small>. W. H. BOURNE. Shell wound, on Cambrai Road, near Tilloy, April 18, 1917. To U.K.

21186 G<small>NR</small>. P. CALLAGAN. Shell wound, on Cambrai Road, near Tilloy, April 18, 1917. To U.K.

52556 G<small>NR</small>. A. THOMPSON. Shell wound, on Cambrai Road, near Tilloy, April 18, 1917. To U.K.

90103 G<small>NR</small>. H. RONSON. Gunshot wound, foot, on Cambrai Road, near Tilloy, April 18, 1917. To U.K.

88336 G<small>NR</small>. W. BROWN. Killed in action on Cambrai Road, near Tilloy, April 18, 1917.

59292 G<small>NR</small>. L. DAVIES. Killed in action on Cambrai Road, near Tilloy, April 18, 1917.

9493 G<small>NR</small>. J. JONES. Gunshot wound, neck, on Cambrai Road, near Tilloy, April 20, 1917. Died of wounds.

35711 Sergt. T. HILL. Shell wound, leg and face, on Cambrai Road, near Tilloy, April 22, 1917.

79435 Bdr. W. McVEIGH. Shell wound, leg, ankle (right), on Cambrai Road, near Tilloy, April 22, 1917. To U.K.

45058 Gnr. A. SENIOR. Shell wound, on Cambrai Road, near Tilloy, April 25, 1917.

38165 Gnr. I. GREAVES. Shell wound, on Cambrai Road, near Tilloy, April 27, 1917. To U.K.

88306 Gnr. S. BRAY. Shell wound and shell shock, on Cambrai Road, near Tilloy, April 18, 1917. To U.K.

88247 Gnr. H. B. JAMES. Gunshot wound, shoulder, at Wancourt, May 1, 1917. To U.K.

51251 Gnr. J. WHALE. Gunshot wounds, head, chest, at Wancourt, May 1, 1917. Died of wounds.

44662 Act. Bdr. J. PEACOCK. Gunshot wound, arm and leg, at Wancourt, May 4, 1917.

37791 Act. Bdr. S. GREY. Gunshot wound, hand, at Wancourt, May 12, 1917.

44942 Corpl. F. GOSDEN. Killed in action, at Wancourt, May 16, 1917.

75394 Gnr. F. WHITE. Gunshot wound, right hand, on Cambrai Road, near Tilloy, May 22, 1917.

Major C. PEARSON. Gunshot wound, hand, at Wancourt, May 3, 1917. To U.K.

ROLL OF HONOUR

93402 GNR. H. BISHOP. Gunshot wound, neck, at Oost Dunkerque, July 26, 1917. To U.K.

88269 GNR. C. E. LIDDELL. Gunshot wound, forehead, at Oost Dunkerque, August 7, 1917. To U.K.

2ND LIEUT. A. W. B. PEGGIE. Killed in action, at Oost Dunkerque, August 17, 1917.

2ND LIEUT. P. R. PURDIE. Severely wounded, at Oost Dunkerque, August 17, 1917. Died of wounds, August 17, 1917.

2ND LIEUT. T. M. WITHEROW. Gassed, at Nieuport Bains, August, 1917. To Base. Rejoined November, 1917.

296375 GNR. C. HOWARD. Gunshot wound, leg, at Oost Dunkerque, August 25, 1917. To U.K.

280458 GNR. J. DWYER. Gunshot wound, at Oost Dunkerque, August 25, 1917. To U.K.

56487 ACT. BDR. W. FRIEND. Gunshot wound, knee, at Oost Dunkerque, August 29, 1917. To U.K.

44905 BDR. P. HOBDEN. Gunshot wound, at Oost Dunkerque, August 29, 1917. Remained at duty.

316475 GNR. S. A. DAWSON. Killed in action, at Coxyde Bains, September 4, 1917.

43995 ACT. BDR. J. BELL. Gunshot wounds, wrist and arm, at Oost Dunkerque, September 1, 1917.

45048 GNR. J. COCKBURN. Gunshot wounds, arm (left), leg and thigh, at Oost Dunkerque, September 4, 1917. To U.K.

53090 GNR. H. NEWMAN. Gunshot wound, at Oost Dunkerque, September 4, 1917. Died of wounds.

68471 GNR. J. J. ANDERSON. Enemy bomb, scalp wound, at Coxyde Bains, September 4, 1917.

52882 GNR. A. FINK. Enemy bomb, buttock and knee, at Coxyde Bains, September 4, 1917. To U.K.

112198 GNR. H. TELFORD. Enemy bomb, buttock and knee, at Coxyde Bains, September 4, 1917. To U.K.

107703 GNR. J. H. WALFORD. Gunshot wound, buttock, at Oost Dunkerque, September 7, 1917. To U.K.

32176 SERGT. A. THOMAS. Gunshot wound, head, at Oost Dunkerque, September 7, 1917. To U.K.

16131 GNR. D. T. VINCETT. Gunshot wound, at Oost Dunkerque, September 7, 1917. To U.K.

66900 GNR. H. E. PERRY. Gunshot wound, at Oost Dunkerque, September 7, 1917. To U.K.

45054 CORPL. W. WADDINGTON, M.M. Gunshot wound leg (right), at Oost Dunkerque, September 7, 1917. To U.K. Awarded M.M. Rejoined December 27, 1917.

ROLL OF HONOUR

93665 Gnr. P. SMITH. Gunshot wounds, face and chest, at Oost Dunkerque, September 5, 1917. To U.K.

308909 Gnr. R. BAKER. Gunshot wound, leg (right), at Oost Dunkerque, September 12, 1917.

76219 Act. Bdr. J. C. ADCOCK. Killed in action, at Oost Dunkerque, September 7, 1917.

132773 Gnr. T. R. RICE. Killed in action, at Oost Dunkerque, September 7, 1917.

46436 Sergt. R. W. HILL. Gunshot wound, face, at Oost Dunkerque, September 12, 1917. Remained at duty.

308076 Gnr. T. BOWEN. Gunshot wound, at Oost Dunkerque, October 12, 1917. To U.K.

41768 Gnr. G. HARRISON. Gunshot wound, at Nieuport Bains, October 9, 1917. Remained at duty.

100925 Gnr. J. K. McFARLANE. Gunshot wound, at Oost Dunkerque, October 9, 1917. Remained at duty.

280427 Gnr. J. PICKWELL. Gunshot wound, at Oost Dunkerque, October 9, 1917. Died of wounds.

44989 Gnr. H. DOVER. Gunshot wound, at Oost Dunkerque, October 12, 1917. Rejoined unit November 12, 1917.

46436 Sergt. R. W. HILL. Gunshot wound, shoulder, at Oost Dunkerque, October 15, 1917. Second time. To U.K.

58735 Gnr. J. LEDGUARD. Gunshot wound, chest, at Oost Dunkerque, October 26, 1917. To U.K.

39492 Sergt. C. PHILLIMORE. Slightly wounded, at Souastre Fork, March 28, 1918. Remained at duty.

45513 L. Bdr. H. CULF. Slightly wounded, at Souastre Fork, March 28, 1918. Remained at duty.

54624 Gnr. D. MORGAN. Shell wound, leg (left), shoulder (right), at Souastre Fork, April 2, 1918. To U.K.

93185 Dr. R. SHRIMPTON. Gunshot wound, shoulder (left), Souastre Village, April 5, 1918. To U.K.

52440 L. Bdr. C. HARRISON. Slightly wounded, at Souastre Fork, April 5, 1918. Remained at duty.

54984 Sergt. D. STREET. Slightly wounded, at Souastre Fork, April 11, 1918. Remained at duty.

45145 Gnr. H. MURPHY. Slightly wounded, at Souastre Fork, April 20, 1918. Remained with unit.

88428 Gnr. A. PALMER. Slightly wounded, shoulder, at Souastre Road, April 22, 1918. Remained with unit.

106300 Gnr. A. ENTWISTLE. Wounded, hand (amputated thumb), at Souastre Fork, April 25, 1918. To U.K. May 1, 1918.

44919 Gnr. S. KIME. Slightly wounded, at Hannescamp, May 9, 1918. Remained with unit.

124178 Sergt. D. DAVIES. Gunshot wound, back, at Hannescamp, May 31, 1918. To U.K. June 5, 1918.

280703 Corpl. W. C. WOOTTEN (M.M.). Slightly wounded, elbow (right), May 31, 1918. Returned to unit from hospital.

60946 Gnr. S. H. SIMS. Slightly wounded, leg, at Hannescamp, June 18, 1918. Remained with unit.

88179 Gnr. W. MORRISON. Severely wounded, head, at Hannescamp, June 15, 1918. Died from wounds received in action, June 19, 1918.

45016 Dr. R. BURNHAM. Gunshot wound, leg (left), thigh (left), arm, at Hannescamp, June 16, 1918. Invalided to U.K., June 23, 1918.

41745 Corpl. W. R. ADAMS (M.M.). Slightly wounded, leg, at Hannescamp, July 16, 1918. Invalided to U.K., August 19, 1918.

48169 L. Bdr. M. O'DRISCOLL. Gunshot wound, arm, at Hannescamp, August 11, 1918. Remained with unit.

311289 Gnr. W. POTTER. Slightly wounded, leg and arm, at Bucquoy, August 22, 1918. Invalided to U.K. August 26, 1918.

204177 Gnr. C. CAVE. Slightly wounded, thigh (right), at Bucquoy, August 22, 1918. Invalided to U.K. August 26, 1918.

44965 Corpl. J. COWEY. Severely wounded, head, at Achiet-le-Petit, August 28, 1918. Died of wounds received in action, August 29, 1918.

291751 Gnr. J. CASTLE. Gunshot wound, forearm, at Bucquoy, August 21, 1918. Invalided to U.K. August 27, 1918.

44646 Bdr. P. HARDS. Gunshot wound, arm (right), at O.P., August 22, 1918. Invalided to U.K. August 29, 1918.

76254 Gnr. A. T. BRADSHAW. Gunshot wounds, multiple, at Bucquoy, August 26, 1918. Invalided to U.K. August 30, 1918.

56541 Dr. E. GILL. Gunshot wound, leg (left), at Achiet-le-Petit, August 28, 1918. Invalided to U.K. September 1, 1918.

70354 Dr. C. J. MAHONEY. Gunshot wound, cheek, at Achiet-le-Petit, August 28, 1918. Invalided to U.K. September 1, 1918.

44653 Bdr. A. ALCOCK. Wounds and burns from explosion, at Achiet-le-Petit, August 26, 1918. Invalided to U.K. August 30, 1918.

44959 CORPL. J. METCALFE. Slightly hit, forehead, at Ruyaulcourt, September 6, 1918. Invalided to U.K. September 9, 1918.

308909 GNR. R. BAKER. Severely wounded, arm and side, at Ruyaulcourt, September 6, 1918. Invalided to U.K. September 10, 1918.

163753 GNR. B. J. C. CHESTERMAN. Contused shoulder (left), at Ruyaulcourt, September 6, 1918. Invalided to U.K. September 10, 1918.

295855 GNR. J. W. WILKINSON. Gunshot wound, abdomen, at Ruyaulcourt, September 20, 1918. Invalided to U.K. September 24, 1918.

54984 SERGT. STREET D. Gunshot wound, face, at Neuville, September 27, 1918. To England October 1, 1918.

27041 SERGT. DALE B. (M.M.). Gunshot wound, head, at Metz-au-Couture, September 27, 1918.

49365 GNR. J. SEARSON. Slightly wounded, at Metz-au-Cou-ture, September 27, 1918. Remained with unit on duty.

310388 GNR. R. ELLIS. Slightly wounded, arm, at Metz-au-Couture, October 29, 1918. Invalided to England November 10, 1918.

41728 BDR. S. MILES. Gas shell wound, at Romeries, October 21, 1918.

60946 Gnr. S. SIMS. Gas shell wound, at Romeries, October 21, 1918.

80901 Gnr. C. A. WILLIAMSON. Gas shell wound, at Romeries, October 21, 1918.

116852 Gnr. F. W. CORBETT. Gunshot wound, leg (left), at Metz-au-Couture, October 20, 1918. Invalided to England October 28, 1918.

43734 L. Bdr. J. LEE. Gunshot wounds, arm (right) and side, at Romeries, October 29, 1918.

45036 Corpl. T. MEEHAN. Slightly wounded, arm (left), at Romeries, October 29, 1918.

90624 Dr. H. CLARKE. Gunshot wounds, eye (left) and arm (left), at Romeries, November 1, 1918. Invalided to England November 1, 1918.

275663 Gnr. T. EDWARDS. Slightly wounded, arm (left), face and thigh, at Romeries, October 29, 1918. Invalided to England November 3, 1918.

HONOURS AND AWARDS

Officers, N.C.O.s and Men Decorated or Mentioned in Despatches

52705 GNR. A. M. EVERETT, M.M., May 19, 1916. During a German aeroplane shoot on a battery on the outskirts of Bienvillers-au-Bois, some R.F.A. drivers attempting to pass were hit by a shell, one being killed and one wounded seriously. Gnr. Everett, in spite of the shelling, carried this man to a place of safety, thence handing him over to be dressed. He only could do so at very great personal risk. B.C. staff.

LIEUT. J. F. YOUNG, mentioned in dispatches, June, 1916. B.C. staff.

44917 A. BDR. A. R. MUIR, M.M., and 41747 GNR. W. R. ADAMS, M.M., June 24, 1916. On 2nd Lieut. P. D. Sanders being wounded in

O.P. facing Ovillers (Somme) these two men, with entire disregard for their own safety, carried their officer practically from the front line across the open, in full view of the German lines, to the dressing station. B.C. staff.

41689 Corp. W. W. HOLNESS, M.M., July 6, 1916. Due to back firing, caused by a defective tube or vent, cartridges were set alight in No. 3 (enclosed) emplacement at Martinsart (Somme). A sergeant and some gunners were badly burned. One man remained in the ammunition recess, which was still burning. Corporal Holness, in spite of the heat and the fumes, dragged this man out of the recess to safety, doing so at very great risk. C Sub-section.

27041 Bdr. B. DALE, M.M., and 45513 Gnr. H. CULF, M.M., November 15, 1916. During some two hours' continuous shelling with gas shell on the Battery when in position near Pozieres, one shell penetrated into the B.C. post, gassing and wounding 2nd Lieut. Denison and the telephonist on duty. These two men, though almost overcome by the fumes, nevertheless succeeded in getting both officer and telephonist from beneath the debris. Bdr. Dale, A Sub-section; Gnr. Culf, C Sub-section.

Captain P. S. WILTSHIRE, mentioned in dispatches, Honours List, January, 1917. Battery Commander.

HONOURS AND AWARDS

1852 B.S.M. A. G. COOPER, D.C.M., awarded June 4, 1917. Continued good service to Battery between September, 1914, and March, 1917. B.S.M.

2ND LIEUT. C. R. HODGKINSON, mentioned in dispatches, June, 1917. Right section.

45054 CORPL. W. WADDINGTON, M.M., September 7, 1917. During shelling of Battery near Oost Dunkerque (coastal sector), ammunition set alight and some casualties caused. Corpl. Waddington, though himself wounded, refused to have his own wound attended to until those of the others had been attended to, and gave every assistance. E Sub-section.

2ND LIEUT. C. H. SCOTT, M.C., and 36711 SERGT. S. JACKSON, M.M., November 11, 1917. During very heavy observed shelling on No. 2 gun, near Oost Dunkerque, Lieut. Scott and Sergt. Jackson went out immediately in front of the gun, and by keeping smoke candles burning for some two hours till dusk, put the M.P.I. of the German guns short, thus saving the guns without doubt. 250 rounds at least fired, and the smoke candles were only kept going under a rain of splinters. Centre Section.

MAJOR R. A. WATSON, M.C., mentioned in dispatches, Honours List, January, 1918; D.S.O., Honours List, June 2, 1919. Battery Commander.

41502 B.Q.M.S. W. E. McVEIGH, Meritorious Service Medal, Honours List, January, 1918. Continuous good service to Battery between September, 1914, and November, 1917. B.Q.M.S.

MAJOR CECIL PEARSON, M.C., Honours List, January, 1918. Continuous good service in Battery between October, 1916 and May 3, 1917, on which date he was wounded. Battery Commander.

SERGT. R. W. HILL, Decoration Militaire (Belgian), February 3, 1918. For gallant services rendered on Belgian coast between July and October, 1917. B Sub-section.

2ND LIEUT. W. J. BAIRD, M.C., April 5, 1918; 280703 CORPL. W. C. WOOTTEN, M.M., April 5, 1918; 42145 CORPL. W. J. HOLMAN, M.M., April 5, 1918—for gallant services and coolness under shell fire. Corpl. W. C. Wootten, D Sub-section; Corpl. W. J. Holman, E Sub-section.

LIEUT. E. W. SPALDING, M.C., June 3, 1918, and BDR. P. HARDS, D.C.M., June 3, 1918. For continuous good services to Battery and gallantry between July, 1916, and May, 1918 (O.P. duties). Bdr. P. Hards, B.C. Staff.

L. BDR. S. WILLIAMS, M.M., August 12, 1918. For gallant action on the road between Bienvillers and Hannescamp on August 7, 1918 (a direct hit on G.S. wagon and team by enemy), getting wounded men and horses away under heavy enemy shell fire. B Sub-section.

2ND LIEUT. W. J. BAIRD, Bar to M.C., September, 1918. For continuous good services to Battery and gallantry on the advance from August 21, 1918 (O.P. duties). B.C. Staff.

2ND LIEUT. S. C. PETRIE, M.C., September, 1918. For continuous good services at O.P. during advance, August 21, 1918, and gallant action in personally carrying wounded observer (Bdr. Hards P., D.C.M.) under heavy enemy shell fire, at great risk, to a dressing station. R Section.

CAPTAIN G. H. BISHOP, mentioned in dispatches, November 8, 1918.

294110 CORPL. W. A. BLOOR, mentioned in dispatches, November 8, 1918. Awarded "Belgian Decoration Militaire" December 7, 1918. For attending wounded under shell fire and continuous good service and devotion to duty as B.C.'s Assistant.

49583 FARR. STAFF SERGT. F. PAYNE, M.M., February 14, 1919. For gallantry and good work during the advance in 1918. Peace dispatch.

ROLL OF OFFICERS

Who have served with the Battery

Lieut. REID (Regular). Joined October, 1914; left October, 1914.

Major C. W. COLLINGWOOD (Regular). Joined October, 1914; left October, 1914. 1917 B.G.H.A. 15th Corps.

Major TAYLOR (Regular). Joined October 18, 1914; left October 26, 1914.

Captain NIVEN (Regular). Joined October 26, 1914; left October 29, 1914. Posted to command 10 H.B.

2nd Lieut. J. R. DAVIES (Special Reserve). Joined 26 October, 1914; left January 10, 1915. Posted to 90 H.B.—later in 109—took Regular Commission—gained M.C.

2nd Lieut., Lieut., Captain J. F. YOUNG (Temporary). Joined October 27, 1914; left April 8, 1918. Lieutenant January 1, 1916—Captain December 12, 1916. Transferred to 262 S.B.

ROLL OF OFFICERS

MAJOR C. N. BUZZARD (Regular). Joined October 28, 1914; left November 28, 1914. Posted to 90 H.B.—later Brevet Lieut.-Colonel—Gallipoli, France, Italy (1917).

2ND LIEUT. C. W. D. WARD (Temporary). Joined October 30, 1914; left September 21, 1915. To 114 H.B.—latterly relinquished commission.

2ND LIEUT. D. T. THOMSON (Temporary). Joined October 30, 1914; left February 8, 1915. To Coast Defence.

CAPTAIN SMYTHE (Regular). Joined November 28, 1914; left December 3, 1914. Promoted Major and posted to Coast Defence, Harwich.

CAPTAIN H. WILSON (Temporary). Joined November 30, 1914; left December 12, 1915. To England.

MAJOR EVAN-SMITH (Temporary). Joined December 3, 1914; left January 26, 1915. Relinquishes commission.

LIEUT. B. L. GILLING (Temporary). Joined December 7, 1914; left January 7, 1915.

LIEUT. E. J. E. BOYS (Temporary). Joined January 7, 1915; left February 3, 1915. To 71 H.B.—later awarded M.C.—transferred to R.E.

LIEUT., CAPTAIN W. J. O. STUDD (Temporary). Joined February 7, 1915; left August 26, 1916. Captain November 29, 1915—evacuated from Battery to England—sick.

2ND LIEUT. W. L. EASTWICK-FIELD (Regular). Joined February 7, 1915; left June 5, 1915. Evacuated, sick, to England—later in 146 H.B.—awarded M.C.

MAJOR R. A. THOMAS (Regular). Joined February 11, 1915; left December 28, 1915. To Ordnance Committee, Woolwich—later made Brevet Lieut.-Colonel.

2ND LIEUT. J. V. WISCHER (Special Reserve). Joined June 30, 1915; left February 27, 1916. Seconded to R.F.C.—afterwards posted missing.

2ND LIEUT. W. S. A. JONES (Special Reserve). Joined July 3, 1915; left August 6, 1915. To 16th Brigade R.G.A. as Orderly Officer.

2ND LIEUT. MOODY (Temporary). Joined August 6, 1915; left March 4, 1916. From 9 H.B.—evacuated, sick, to England.

2ND LIEUT. J. K. IRVINE (Special Reserve). Joined December 4, 1915; left April 15, 1916. To 9 H.B.—later wounded.

2ND LIEUT. D. BRICE (Special Reserve). Joined December 24, 1915; left May 5, 1917. Evacuated, sick, to England.

CAPTAIN P. S. WILTSHIRE (Regular). Joined January 24, 1916; left December 15, 1916. Evacuated, sick, to England—later to Mesopotamia with Siege Battery as Major.

2ND LIEUT. SLOANE-STANLEY (Special Reserve). Joined February 12, 1916; left March 25, 1916. To 16th Group as Orderly Officer—later with 108 H.B.

LIEUT. G. E. MULLIS (Regular). Joined April 15, 1916; killed in action, September 30, 1916. Posted from 9 H.B.—buried in Aveluy churchyard (Somme).

2ND LIEUT. CROUCH (Regular). Joined May 10, 1916; left May 28, 1916. To 133 H.B.

2ND LIEUT., LIEUT. C. R. HODGKINSON (Regular). Joined May 15, 1916; left September, 1917. To Ordnance Course, England.

2ND LIEUT., LIEUT. P. D. SANDERS (Special Reserve). Joined May 15, 1916; posted to 1/1 Kents, March 5, 1918. Wounded June 24, 1916—rejoined 1917—Lieutenant July 1, 1917.

2ND LIEUT., LIEUT. E. W. SPALDING, M.C. (Temporary). Joined July 7, 1916; appointed Second in Command 103 Siege Battery, September 9, 1918. Lieutenant July 1, 1917; promoted Captain September 9, 1918.

2ND LIEUT. DU HEAUME (Special Reserve). Joined July 30, 1916; left August 18, 1916. To 24 H.B.

LIEUT., CAPTAIN, MAJOR C. PEARSON (Temporary). Joined October 2, 1916; wounded May 3, 1917. Joined from 122 H.B.—Captain October 2, 1916—Major December 12, 1916—awarded M.C. January, 1918.

ROLL OF OFFICERS

2ND LIEUT. C. D. DENISON (Special Reserve). Joined October 2, 1916; wounded and gassed November 15, 1916. Joined with section of 172 H.B.

2ND LIEUT. A. W. B. PEGGIE (Territorial). Joined March 6, 1917; killed in action August 17, 1917. Buried in Coxyde cemetery, Belgium.

2ND LIEUT. P. R. PURDIE (Special Reserve). Joined March 13, 1917; killed in action August 17, 1917. Buried in Coxyde cemetery, Belgium.

MAJOR R. A. WATSON, M.C. and Bar (Regular). Joined May 6, 1917. From 35 H.B.

LIEUT. G. H. BISHOP (Temporary). Joined May, 1917; left June 28, 1918. Promoted Acting Captain and posted to 1/1 Kents, and took over Second in Command. Rejoined November 12, 1918, as Second in Command.

LIEUT. T. M. WITHEROW (Regular). Joined August, 1917. Evacuated, sick, August, 1917—rejoined November, 1917—promoted Lieut. December 6, 1918.

LIEUT. R. BROMLEY (Special Reserve). Joined August 31, 1917; left April 7, 1918. Evacuated, sick, to England. Rejoined October 17, 1918, from Winchester.

LIEUT. C. H. SCOTT, M.C. (Special Reserve). Joined August, 1917. Promoted Lieut. July 3, 1918.

LIEUT. S. C. PETRIE, M.C. (Special Reserve). Joined September, 1917. Promoted Lieut. November 27, 1918.

2ND LIEUT. W. J. BAIRD, M.C. and Bar (Special Reserve). Joined January 24, 1918.

CAPTAIN H. H. HUTCHINSON, M.C. (Temporary). Joined April 7, 1918; left October 1, 1918. From 127 H.B.—evacuated, sick, to England, October 1, 1918.

2ND LIEUT. E. HANSON (Temporary). Joined May 5, 1918.

2ND LIEUT. M. FITZGERALD (Temporary). Joined June 14, 1918. Commissioned from Sergt. and posted in his own unit.

2ND LIEUT. H. DOWNES (Special Reserve). Joined August 12, 1918; left November 27, 1918. Evacuated, sick, November 27, 1918, to England.

2ND LIEUT. W. SPENCER (Temporary). Joined October 23, 1918.

CAPTAIN H. J. MORTIMER, M.C. (Regular). Joined February 28, 1919; posted to 129 H.B. April 9, 1919.

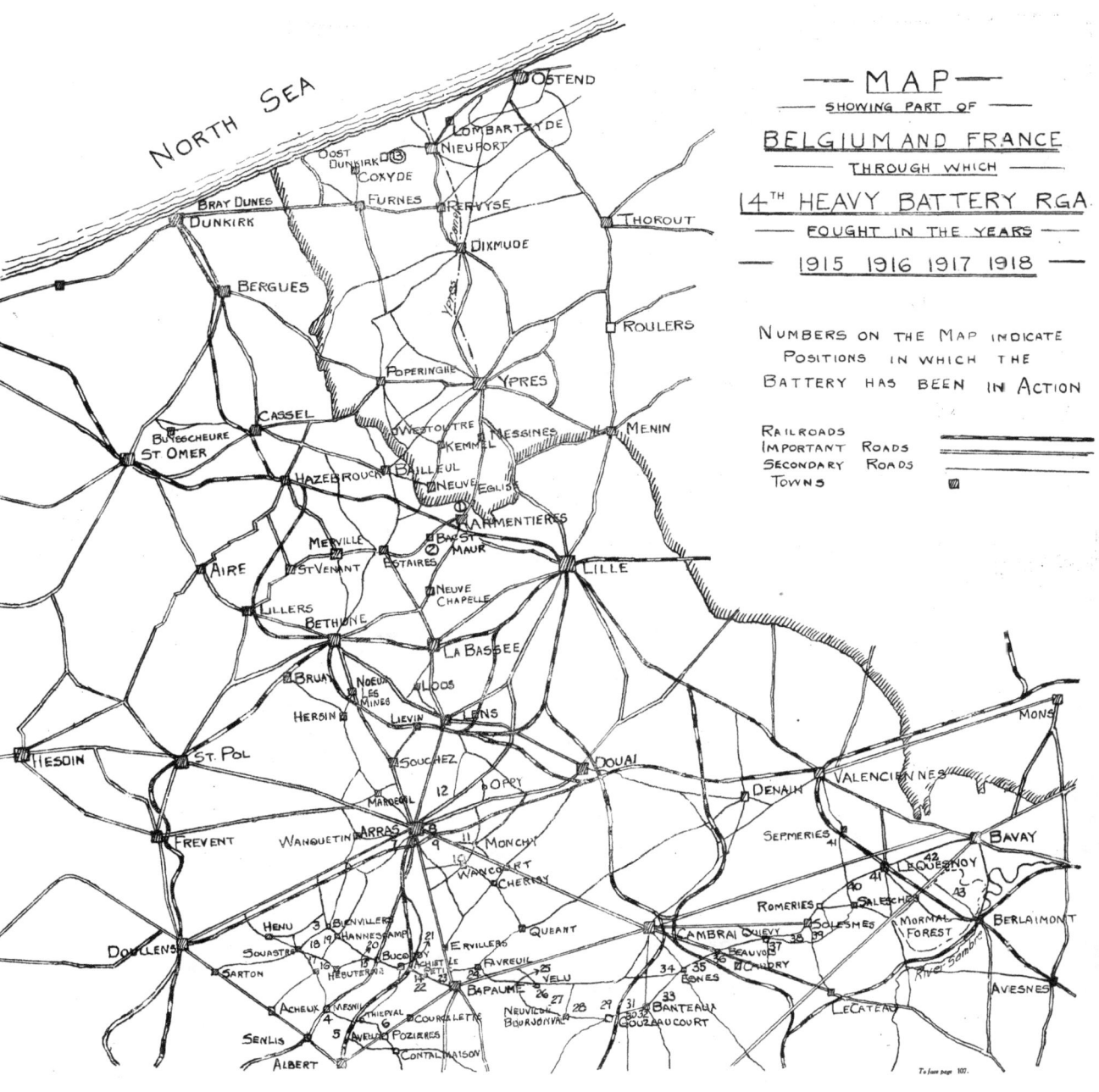

INDEX TO POSITIONS NUMBERED ON MAP

No.	Place.	Date. From.	To.
1	CLEF DE HOLLANDE.	9–6–15	4–9–15
2	BAC ST. MAUR	4–9–15	1–11–15
3	BIENVILLERS	9–11–15	1–6–16
4	MARTINSART	15–6–16	20–7–16
5	AVELUY	20–7–16	6–10–16
6	POZIERES	6–10–16	8–1–17
7	FAUBOURG D'AMIENS (ARRAS)	27–2–17	9–4–17
8	FAUBOURG ST. SAUVEUR	9–4–17	11–4–17
9	CAMBRAI ROAD	11–4–17	30–4–17
10	WANCOURT	30–4–17	22–5–17
11	FEUCHY CHAPELLE	22–5–17	18–6–17
12	PT. DU JOUR	22–6–17	8–7–17
13	OOST DUNKERKE	10–7–17	4–12–17
14	ACHIET LE GRAND	23–3–18	24–3–18
15	BUCQUOY	25–3–18	25–3–18
16	SAILLY-AU-BOIS	25–3–18	26–3–18
17	SOUASTRE FORK (Chateau de la Haie)	26–3–18	11–5–18
18	WILLOW PATCH (Bienvillers)	11–5–18	31–5–18
19	HANNESCAMP	31–5–18	21–8–18
20	BUCQUOY	21–8–18	24–8–18
21	ACHIET LE PETIT	24–8–18	26–8–18
22	BIHUCOURT	26–8–18	29–8–18
23	BIEFVILLIERS	29–8–18	30–8–18
24	FAVREUIL	30–8–18	3–9–18
25	FREMICOURT	3–9–18	4–9–18
26	VELU WOOD	4–9–18	7–9–18
27	RUYAULCOURT	7–9–18	10–9–18
28	NEUVILLE BOURJONVAL	10–9–18	27–9–18
29	METZ	27–9–18	30–9–18

INDEX TO POSITIONS ON MAP

No.	Place.	From.	To.
30	Gonnelieu	30-9-18	3-10-18
31	Hindenburg Support	3-10-18	7-10-18
32	Banteaux	7-10-18	8-10-18
33	Cheneux Wood	8-10-18	9-10-18
34	Esnes	9-10-18	10-10-18
35	Beauvois (½ Battery)	10-10-18	11-10-18
36	Fontaine-au-Pire (½ Battery)	10-10-18	11-10-18
37	Quievy	11-10-18	20-10-18
38	Fme. au Tertre	20-10-18	22-10-18
39	Briastre	22-10-18	24-10-18
40	Trousse Minou	24-10-18	4-11-18
41	Fme. Ft. St. Martin (4 guns)	4-11-18	5-11-18
41A	Sepmeries (2 guns)	2-11-18	5-11-18
42	Villerau	5-11-18	6-11-18
43	Mormal Forest	6-11-18	11-11-18

Printed in Great Britain for Robert Scott, *Publisher,* Paternoster Row, London, *by* Butler & Tanner, Frome

www.ingramcontent.com/pod-product-compliance
Lightning Source LLC
Chambersburg PA
CBHW080444110426

42743CB00016B/3276